# Make It Take It Crafts

Enelle Eder

Exploring Nature

This book is dedicated to Grace Pulham. Thanks, Mom, for your help, support, encouragement, ideas, inspiration and love. Any accomplishments I have made can be traced back to you!

MAKE IT • TAKE IT CRAFTS/EXPLORING NATURE
©2001 by Rainbow Publishers, second printing
ISBN 1-58411-005-8
Rainbow reorder # RB38024

Rainbow Books
P.O. Box 261129
San Diego, CA 92196

Illustrator: Chuck Galey

Scriptures are from the *Holy Bible: New International Version* (North American Edition), ©1973, 1978, 1984 by the International Bible Society. Used by permission of Zondervan Bible Publishers.

All rights reserved.

*Printed in the United States of America*

# Make It Take It Crafts

## Exploring Nature

**These pages may be copied.**
Permission is granted to the buyer of this book to reproduce, duplicate or photocopy students materials in this book for use with pupils in Sunday school or Bible teaching classes.

Rainbow Books

# Table of Contents

Memory Verse Index .................7
Note to Families .................9
Introduction.................11

## Ages 5-8

Beaver .................16
   Toothpick Beaver Dam .................17
Brook .................19
   Crepe Paper Brook .................20
Bulbs and Seeds .................21
   Seed Gardens .................22
Caterpillars .................27
   Egg Carton Critters .................28
Clouds and Storms.................32
   Clever Cloud Magnet .................33
Fruit .................45
   Juicy Fruit Match Game .................46
Garden of Eden.................48
   Forbidden Fruit Trees .................49
Moon .................54
   Marble Painted Moon .................55
Palm Tree .................57
   Cut 'N' Twist Palm Tree .................58
Raccoon .................59
   Robber Raccoon Mask .................60
Rain.................62
   Colorful Cut 'N' Glue Umbrellas....63
Tares and Weeds.................87
   Weeds Jigsaw Puzzle .................88
Tree by Water .................91
   Towering Tree Sponge Painting ......92
Vine.................94
   Fruitful Grape Clusters .................95

## Ages 8-11

Apple Tree.................13
   Fluffy Apple Blossoms.................14
Butterfly.................24
   Splatter Paint Butterfly .................25
Cedars .................29
   Potato Print Cedars .................30
Creation .................35
   Fold-Out Creation Book .................36
Evergreen Tree .................39
   Easter Grass Evergreens .................40
Flower Gardens .................42
   Peaceful Promise Plants .................43
Lily of the Valley .................51
   Fragile Tissue Lilies .................52
Rainbows .................66
   3-D Tissue Rainbow .................67
Rocks .................69
   Rock Head Family .................70
Roses.................71
   Fold 'N' Peel Roses .................72
Springs .................74
   Hanging Bottle Planter .................75
Stars .................77
   Shining Star Mobile .................78
Sun .................81
   Sun Catcher Sun .................82
Sunflower .................84
   Fold 'N' Cut Sunflower .................85

**Make It • Take It • Make It • Take It • Make It • Take It • Make It • Take It**

# Make It • Take It
# Memory Verses

| | | |
|---|---|---|
| Genesis 1:1 | Creation | 35 |
| Genesis 1:16 | Moon | 54 |
| Genesis 9:13 | Rainbows | 66 |
| Exodus 20:15 | Raccoon | 59 |
| Psalm 1:3 | Tree by Water | 91 |
| Psalm 37:23 | Caterpillars | 27 |
| Psalm 62:2 | Rocks | 69 |
| Psalm 68:9 | Rain | 62 |
| Proverbs 15:1 | Apple Tree | 13 |
| Song of Songs 2:1 | Lily of the Valley | 51 |
| Song of Songs 2:12 | Flower Gardens | 42 |
| Isaiah 35:1 | Roses | 71 |
| Amos 2:9 | Cedars | 29 |
| Micah 7:8 | Sunflower | 84 |
| Matthew 2:10 | Stars | 77 |
| Matthew 7:16 | Fruit | 45 |
| Matthew 10:8 | Brook | 19 |
| Matthew 13:30 | Tares and Weeds | 87 |
| Matthew 26:41 | Beaver | 16 |
| Mark 4:39 | Clouds and Storms | 32 |
| John 3:16 | Evergreen Tree | 39 |
| John 4:14 | Springs | 74 |
| John 12:13 | Palm Tree | 57 |
| John 15:5 | Vine | 94 |
| Acts 17:25 | Bulbs and Seeds | 21 |
| 1 Corinthians 15:34 | Garden of Eden | 48 |
| 2 Corinthians 5:17 | Butterfly | 24 |
| Ephesians 4:26 | Sun | 81 |

**Make It • Take It • Make It • Take It • Make It • Take It • Make It • Take It**

## To Families

We have some exciting crafts planned for use in teaching Bible lessons. We would like to ask your help in saving or collecting the following checked items.

- ❏ aluminum pie pans
- ❏ bottles, two-liter soda
- ❏ cereal boxes, single serving size
- ❏ chenille wire
- ❏ coffee grounds
- ❏ construction paper
- ❏ cotton
- ❏ craft foam
- ❏ craft glue
- ❏ craft sticks
- ❏ crayons
- ❏ crepe paper streamers
- ❏ Easter grass
- ❏ egg cartons
- ❏ foam packing chips
- ❏ foam plates
- ❏ glitter
- ❏ glue
- ❏ hole punch
- ❏ ink pads
- ❏ marbles
- ❏ markers, washable and permanent
- ❏ pebbles
- ❏ poster board
- ❏ rocks
- ❏ scissors
- ❏ seeds
- ❏ self-stick plastic, clear
- ❏ tempera paint
- ❏ tissue paper
- ❏ toothpicks
- ❏ yarn

Please bring in the items on _____.

**Thank you for your help!**

---

## To Families

We have some exciting crafts planned for use in teaching Bible lessons. We would like to ask your help in saving or collecting the following checked items.

- ❏ aluminum pie pans
- ❏ bottles, two-liter soda
- ❏ cereal boxes, single serving size
- ❏ chenille wire
- ❏ coffee grounds
- ❏ construction paper
- ❏ cotton
- ❏ craft foam
- ❏ craft glue
- ❏ craft sticks
- ❏ crayons
- ❏ crepe paper streamers
- ❏ Easter grass
- ❏ egg cartons
- ❏ foam packing chips
- ❏ foam plates
- ❏ glitter
- ❏ glue
- ❏ hole punch
- ❏ ink pads
- ❏ marbles
- ❏ markers, washable and permanent
- ❏ pebbles
- ❏ poster board
- ❏ rocks
- ❏ scissors
- ❏ seeds
- ❏ self-stick plastic, clear
- ❏ tempera paint
- ❏ tissue paper
- ❏ toothpicks
- ❏ yarn

Please bring in the items on _____.

**Thank you for your help!**

# Introduction

All children love crafts! However, in today's fast-paced world, a simple coloring project is no longer adequate to hold a child's attention. *Make It • Take It Crafts* is a set of five books that gives you new ideas for teaching important eternal truths. These activities are designed to help you teach your children about God through Bible-based lessons.

Each of the five books contains over 25 different topics to discuss and unique crafts to accompany them. A memory verse, which relates directly to the topic, is provided for each lesson. Encourage the children to write the memory verse on the craft whenever possible as a take-home reminder.

Detailed instructions and full-size, reproducible patterns are included for each craft. And they can be made from household materials or basic craft supplies. A list of supplies is provided on page 9 in a reproducible note format so you can ask for families' assistance in collecting materials.

Each lesson is labeled according to the age appropriateness based on the subject matter and difficulty of the craft. However, use your own judgment as to which lessons and crafts are suitable for the skills and interests of your students. You will find that the lessons can be successfully adapted for use in Sunday school, children's church, vacation Bible school, Christian school or wherever God's Word is taught.

With *Make It • Take It Crafts* your children will not only make and take crafts — they will make new commitments that will take them into a life of serving the Lord.

# Apple Tree

### Ages 8-11

### Memory Verse

*A gentle answer turns away wrath, but a harsh word stirs up anger.*

~**Proverbs 15:1**

## Gentle Apple Trees

Do you know what an orchard is? It is a place where fruit trees grow. What kind of fruit do you like? Today we are going to talk about apple trees. The first thing we usually think about are the sweet, juicy apples the trees give us. God provides apple trees and other kinds of good food so that our bodies can grow strong and healthy. The Bible is our spiritual food.

Have you ever sat under the shade of an apple tree? It provides protection from the heat of the sun on a summer day. That's what it's like when we stay close to Jesus. We don't have to worry about anything, because He will protect us and keep us safe. He will give us peace when problems come into our lives.

When the limbs of an apple tree are shaken violently, the fruit falls hard to the ground and becomes bruised. But carefully picked fruit will remain sweet and useful, just as we need to choose our words carefully when speaking to others. Harsh words will cause bruises that cannot be mended. Be soft spoken and remain sweet.

## For Discussion

**1.** Where do fruit trees grow?
**2.** What do apple trees provide for us?
**3.** How can we "bruise" others with our words?

Make It • Take It • Make It • Take It • Make It • Take It • Make It • Take It

# Fluffy Apple Blossoms

## What You Need

- apple tree patterns from page 15
- 9" x 12" pink construction paper
- white and brown construction paper
- pink tissue paper
- scissors
- pencils
- glue
- markers

## Before Class

Duplicate the apple tree patterns from page 15 for each child.

## What to Do

1. Have each student use the pattern to cut about 10 flowers from white construction paper. They can cut several at a time by folding the paper.

2. Allow the students to cut the pink tissue paper into 1" squares, one per blossom.

3. Show how to drop three or four dabs of glue in the center of each white flower. Wrap one tissue square around the eraser end of a pencil and set it into the glue. The students should repeat this method three or four times for each apple blossom.

4. Have the children use the pattern to cut a limb from brown construction paper using the pattern provided. They should glue it to a sheet of pink construction paper.

5. Instruct the students to write the memory verse on the top of the paper, then glue the apple blossoms to various places on the branch.

Make It • Take It • Make It • Take It • Make It • Take It • Make It • Take It

15

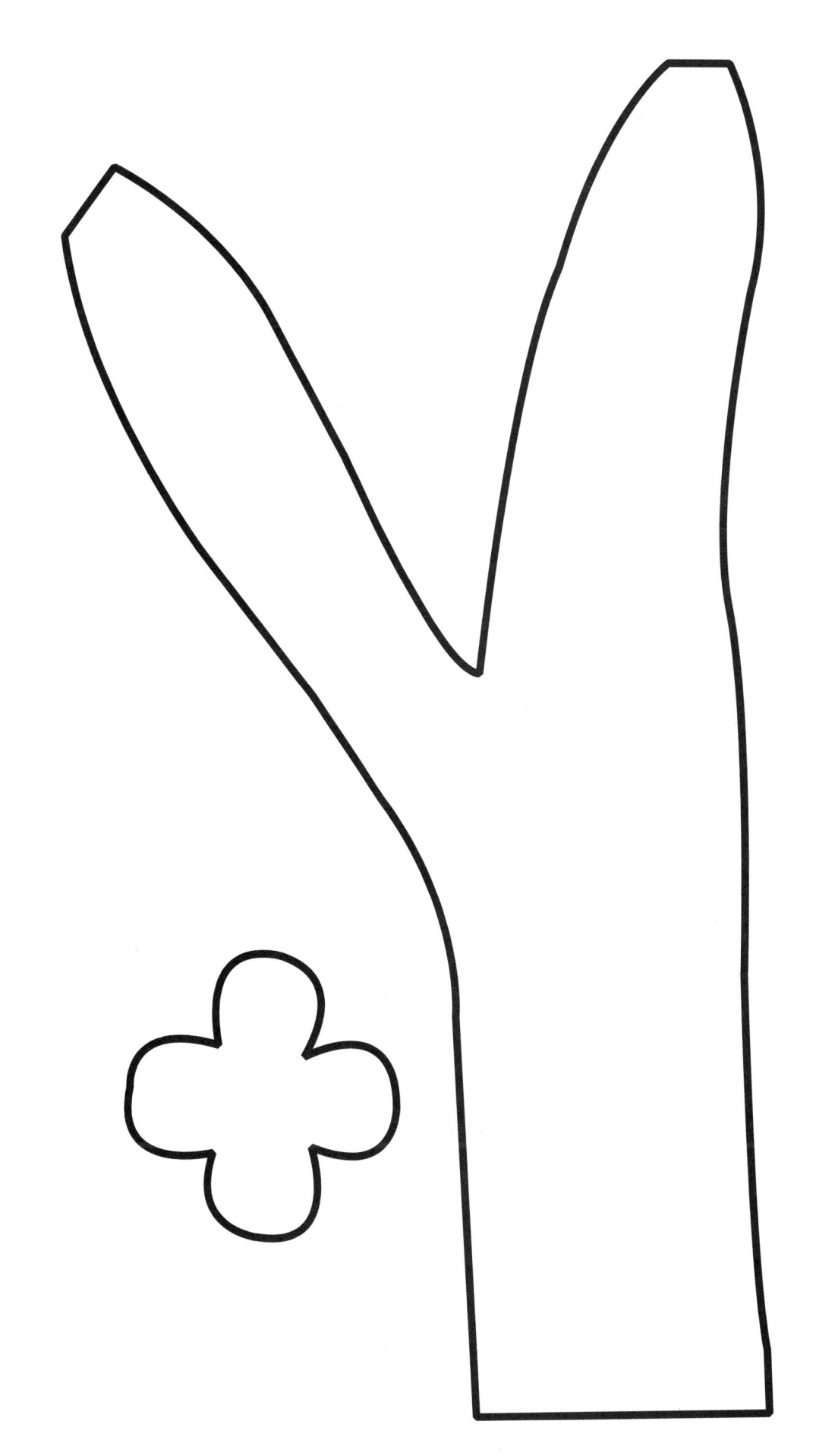

# Beaver

### Ages 5-8

### Memory Verse

*Watch and pray so that you will not fall into temptation.*

~Matthew 26:41

## Watchful Beavers

The beaver is a large, brown rodent that is known for building dams. The beaver is usually 30" long but it stands less than 12" high. It has a broad, flat, scaly tail that is about 10" long. The beaver slaps its wide tail to alert its family of danger. With two long, sharp front teeth, the beaver can cut down trees to widen the area and increase the depth of water around its home, called a lodge.

The beaver works continually to repair and keep up its lodge. The lodge provides a home not only for the beaver's family but for other animals and birds as well, such as wood ducks. Inside the lodge, the beaver stores food for winter. It patrols constantly and watches continually to avoid its predators, including people.

Like the beaver, we need to keep working diligently to make sure our hearts are clean and ready for when Jesus returns. Our homes should be open to those around us who need a helping hand. We, too, have an enemy that is out on the prowl: Satan. But if we are constantly watching, he won't be able to trip us up. We can take a lesson from this furry creature, and always be alert like the beaver.

## For Discussion

1. For what is a beaver known?
2. For what does a beaver watch?
3. Of what enemy do we need to beware?

**Make It • Take It • Make It • Take It • Make It • Take It • Make It • Take It**

# Toothpick Beaver Dam

## What You Need

- beaver from page 18
- poster board
- crayons or construction paper
- toothpicks
- scissors
- glue
- blue markers

*Watch and pray so that you will not fall into temptation.*
Matthew 26:41

## Before Class

Duplicate the beaver from page 18 for each child. Cut the poster board into 8" x 10" pieces, one per child.

## What to Do

1. Have the children cut out and color the beaver brown.

2. Allow them to glue the beaver to one side of the poster board.

3. Give each child a handful of wooden tooth picks and let them construct a beaver lodge, gluing it as they work. (Tell them to break the tooth picks into small pieces when necessary.)

4. Show how to use a blue marker to draw water around the beaver and its lodge.

5. Write or have the students write the memory verse across the top.

*Make It • Take It Crafts*

18

# Brook

### Ages 5-8

### Memory Verse

*Freely you have received, freely give.*
~Matthew 10:8

## Free Flowing Brook

A brook is a small stream of water. There is something very unselfish about a brook. A lake gets its water from streams and run-offs, but a brook gathers ground water and springs to pass on to the larger streams, lakes and seas. The brook exists to give water freely. It asks for nothing in return.

A brook is going somewhere. It is water on a mission! But on its way it doesn't neglect opportunities to be of daily service. A deer can drink of its coolness and kids can dangle their feet in the brook. Where the brook contains a pool, a fisherman can dangle a hook for an unsuspecting trout.

A brook babbles and gurgles as it proceeds on the path it has in life. It almost seems happy.

Service and happiness go together. When we are of service to other people — like the brook — we will be happy. No one who is self-centered is truly happy. We pass through life with heaven as our goal, but we must look for opportunities to help those around us. If we give rather than get, our journeys will be unselfish and we will be truly happy. And God will be happy with us!

## For Discussion

1. Where does a brook get its water?
2. Who benefits from a brook?
3. Name some ways we can be unselfish to others.

Make It • Take It • Make It • Take It • Make It • Take It • Make It • Take It

# Crepe Paper Brook

## What You Need

- poster board
- blue crepe paper streamers
- paint brushes
- scissors
- glue
- markers
- small pebbles

*Freely you have received, freely give.*
Matthew 10:8

## Before Class

Cut the poster board into 8" x 11" pieces, one per child. Cut the blue crepe paper steamers into three 11" lengths per child.

## What to Do

1. Show how to make a line of glue toward the bottom of the poster board to look like waves, then lay a strip of crepe paper in it. Make another glue line in the same manner but overlap the crepe paper slightly. Follow with the third strip.

2. Have the students use a small paint brush and clear water to brush across the crepe paper. They should splash some up over the top edges. (The water will make the crepe paper colors run, and the glue waves stand out.) Caution them not to saturate the paper, but just brush it lightly with water.

3. Allow the students to glue a few pebbles across the brook.

4. Show how to use a black marker to make a few birds in the sky and some minnows in the brook.

5. Remind the students to write the memory verse across the top of the sheet.

Make It • Take It • Make It • Take It • Make It • Take It • Make It • Take It

# Bulbs & Seeds

## Ages 5-8

## Memory Verse

*Because he himself gives all men life.*
~Acts 17:25

## New Seeds of Life

When we want a vegetable or flower garden, we have to plant seeds or bulbs deeply into the ground. If we just lay them on top of the soil, they cannot grow because their source of strength comes from within the dirt. If we just lay them on top of the soil they could also be eaten by birds, blow away in the wind or dry out in the sun. But when they are buried away from the elements of this world into soil — their life-giving source — they emerge as new creations. They no longer look like drab, brown bulbs or seeds. They are fresh and new, ready to fulfill their purposes.

People are like seeds and bulbs. When we are born into this world we are drab and withered from our sinful natures. The longer we stay in the world we become easy prey for the influences of the world. But when we bury our sinful ways in our life-giving source — Jesus Christ — we emerge as beautiful new creatures. We are then ready to fulfill the purpose for which God made us. Our lives are new and fresh. When our roots remain firmly planted, we are able to draw strength daily from Jesus.

## For Discussion

1. Why can't you lay the seeds on top of the soil?
2. What happens when you push the seeds down into the soil?
3. What must we do before we can fulfill God's purpose for us?

**Make It • Take It • Make It • Take It • Make It • Take It • Make It • Take It**

# Seed Gardens

## What You Need

- plant sheet from page 23
- seeds
- crayons
- glue
- stapler
- markers

## Before Class

Duplicate the plant sheet from page 23 for each child. You will need cantaloupe and watermelon seeds, corn and beans.

## What to Do

1. Have the children color the picture with crayons or markers.

2. Show how to fold up the bottom flap and color it brown for soil (to give the sheet durability, you can glue it to construction paper).

3. Give each child two or three of each type of seed. Show how to glue them to the area directly below the appropriate plant.

4. Help the students staple the sides of the folded flap.

5. Write or have the students write the memory verse across the top of the sheet.

*Make It. Take It Crafts*

23

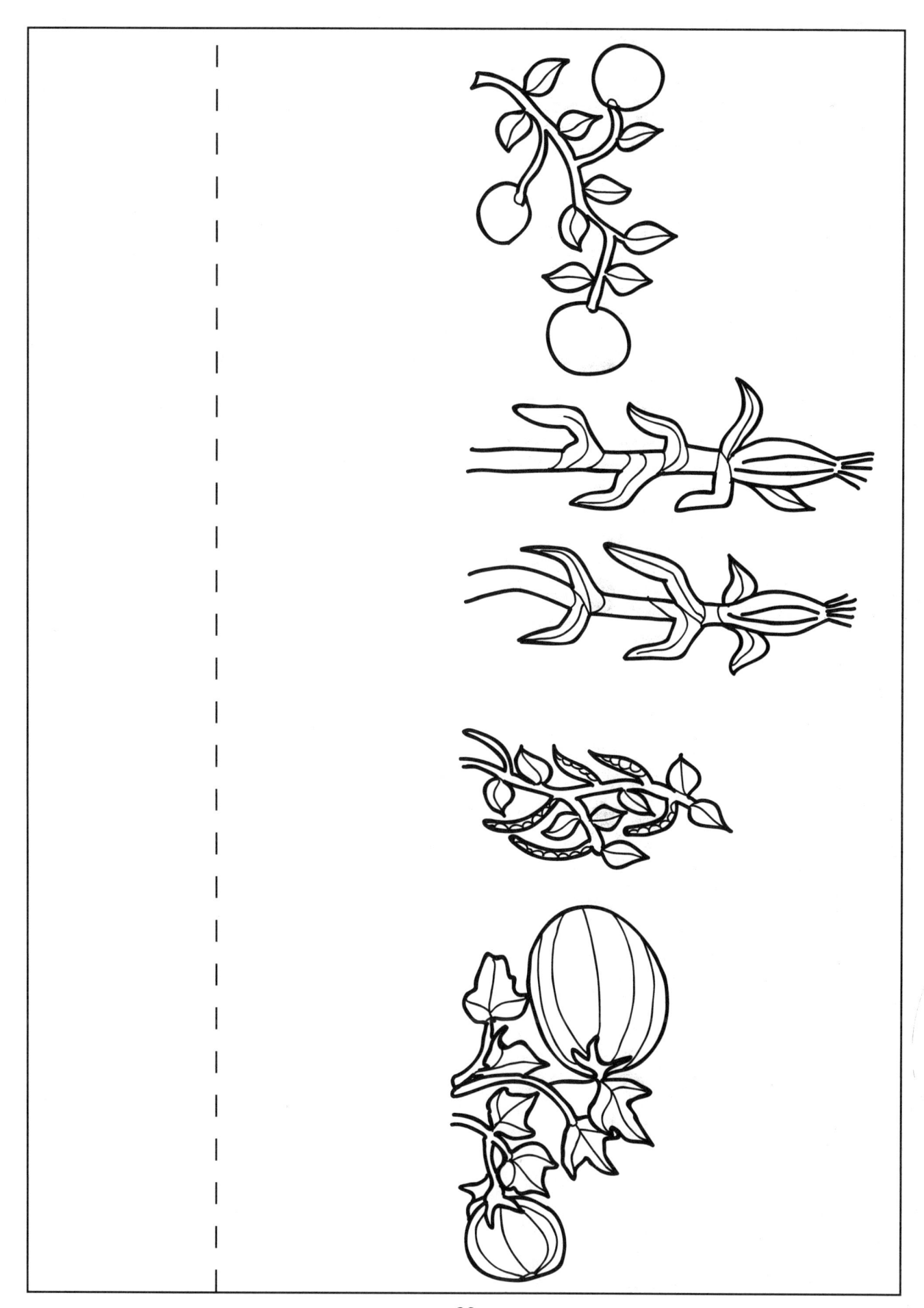

# Butterfly

## Ages 8-11

### Memory Verse

*Therefore, if anyone is in Christ, he is a new creation.*

~2 Corinthians 5:17

## A New Creation

Butterflies are one of nature's most beautiful creatures. They are a member of the insect family. Four stages make up the full life cycle of a butterfly: the egg, the larva or caterpillar, the pupa or cocoon and finally the adult. Butterflies can be found in a variety of habitats, from tundra to rain forests and from below sea level to nearly 20,000 feet in elevation. Butterflies prefer the daylight hours. There are about 18,000 different species world wide.

To become a beautiful adult butterfly, the creature must go through the three stages that are not so pleasant. Only after the butterfly emerges from its dormant state inside the cocoon does it have strong wings to soar through the air.

People are like butterflies. We go through similar stages if we want to emerge as a beautiful new creation called a Christian. Stage one is like an infant, then as we begin to crawl and walk we are like the caterpillar, satisfied to move along close to the earth. Sadly, there are some people who choose to spend their whole lives crawling along in worldly things. But when we begin to desire a better life, we must become dormant to the things of this world by confessing our sins to Jesus. When He forgives us we emerge as beautiful butterflies. Then we are free to soar high above the dirt and filth of the world. We are new creations.

## For Discussion

**1.** Through what four stages does a butterfly go?
**2.** When does it begin to fly?
**3.** How is a Christian a "new creation"?

# Splatter Paint Butterfly

## What You Need

- butterfly patterns from page 26
- construction paper
- tempera paint
- paint brushes
- wiggle eyes
- scissors
- glue
- marker

## Before Class

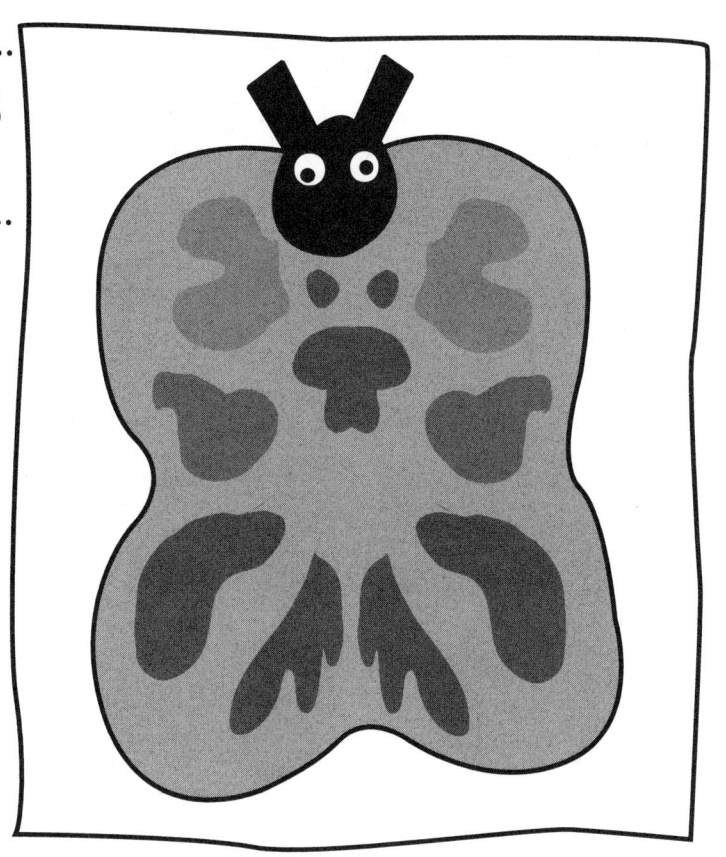

Duplicate the butterfly patterns for each child from page 26. This craft works best with two or three colors of paint.

## What to Do

**1.** Have the children use the pattern to cut a butterfly body from the construction paper color of their choice (not black, however).

**2.** Instruct the students to write the memory verse on the back of the butterfly with a marker.

**3.** Show how to fold the butterfly in half, down the center and open it up again.

**4.** Using a paint brush for each separate color, demonstrate how to dribble paint onto one side of the butterfly. You can make patterns with the drips, but do not brush the paint on the paper.

**5.** Have the students carefully close the butterfly again and press lightly to distribute the colors to the other side. Do not rub or move the paper excessively.

**6.** Instruct the children to open the butterfly carefully and allow the paint to dry.

**7.** Have the students use the pattern to cut the butterfly's head and antennae from black construction paper. Allow them to glue on wiggle eyes. When the butterfly is dry, let the students glue the head to the top center of the body.

26

# Caterpillars

## Ages 5-8

### Memory Verse

*The steps of a good man are ordered by the Lord.*

~Psalm 37:23 KJV

## Purposeful Caterpillars

What is the name of the fuzzy little creature with lots of legs that we see crawling along the ground? It is called a "caterpillar." The caterpillar isn't very strong and it isn't very big. It cannot fly like a majestic eagle. It doesn't provide food like a cow or a chicken. So what is the use of a little caterpillar?

Everything God made has a purpose and a reason for being on earth. The caterpillar is one stage of becoming a butterfly. It moves along, feeding on leaves and grass until it is time for the caterpillar to spin a cocoon around itself. There the caterpillar stays dormant until it emerges as a beautiful butterfly. The caterpillar has then fulfilled its purpose.

Sometimes you might feel like you don't have much purpose, but you do. God created each one of us. We are wonderfully made! We don't all look alike and we aren't all the same size, but God has a special purpose for each of our lives. We must seek Him through prayer and Bible study to find out what our purpose is.

## For Discussion

1. Describe a caterpillar.
2. What is the caterpillar's purpose on earth?
3. How can we know what our purpose is?

**Make It • Take It • Make It • Take It • Make It • Take It • Make It • Take It**

# Egg Carton Critters

## What You Need

- cardboard egg cartons
- green tempera paint
- paint brushes
- paint smocks
- scissors
- glue
- markers
- black chenille wire
- small wiggle eyes

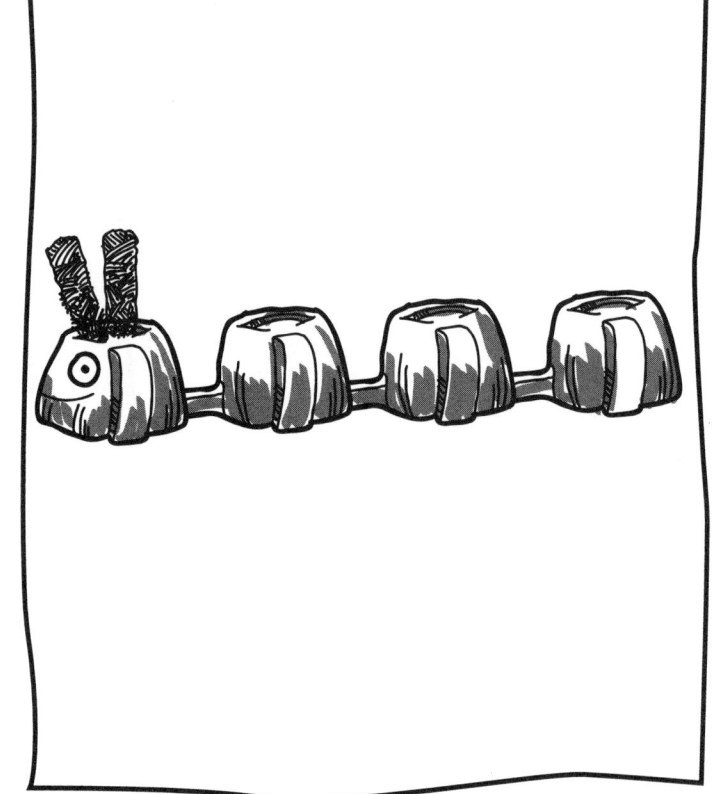

## Before Class

Cut four sections in a row from a paper egg carton for each child. Trim the edges so that the section sets fairly flat. Men's old shirts work well for paint smocks. Cut the chenille wire into one 3" length per child.

## What to Do

1. Have each child wear a paint smock to protect their clothing, then instruct them to paint the entire outside of the carton section with green tempera paint.

2. After the paint has dried, allow the students to glue two wiggle eyes on one end of the section for the head.

3. They should draw on a mouth with a black marker.

4. Give each child a pre-cut length of chenille wire and have them bend it in half for the antennae.

5. Show how to poke a small hole in the top of the head and glue the antennae on.

6. Write or have the students write the memory verse on the side of the caterpillar.

# Cedars

### Ages 8-11

### Memory Verse

*I destroyed the Amorite before them, though he was as tall as the cedars.*

~**Amos 2:9**

## Strong, Tall Cedars

"Cedar" is a common name for three or four species of large trees. They belong to the pine tree family because they have needle-like leaves and their seeds are clustered in cones. Cedars produce fragrant, durable, red-colored wood used in construction and cabinetry.

The best-known cedar is the Cedar of Lebanon mentioned in the Old Testament. The first temple of Solomon was built of this wood. Cedar trees may reach a height of 100 feet. White cedars grow in the swamps of the eastern United States. They are useful sources of timber.

The Christian life can be compared to a cedar tree. We must stand tall and strong in our faith, never ashamed of the gospel. Our words and actions should be fragrant, or pleasing to those around us. Then we can be useful for building the Kingdom of God. Are you like a cedar?

## For Discussion

**1.** Describe a cedar tree.
**2.** In what special way were cedars used in the Bible?
**3.** How can a Christian be like a cedar?

Make It • Take It • Make It • Take It • Make It • Take It • Make It • Take It

# Potato Print Cedars

## What You Need

- tree pattern from page 31
- one medium size potato
- sharp knife
- green tempera paint
- white poster board
- hole punch
- markers
- knives
- yarn
- foam tray

*I destroyed the Amorite before them, though he was as tall as the cedars.*
Amos 2:9

## Before Class

Duplicate the tree pattern from page 31 for each child.

## What to Do

1. Help the students cut a medium size potato in half, lengthwise.

2. Show how to carefully trace one of each of the tree patterns on the two halves.

3. Help the children use a knife to cut away the outer edges of the tree pattern about $1/2$" deep all the way around, leaving a tree "stamp."

4. Give each child a sheet of white poster board. Have them punch two holes in the top center, a few inches apart. Show how to thread a piece of yarn through and tie the ends, making a hanger for the picture.

5. Have the children write the memory verse across the top of the sheet.

6. Pour a small amount of green paint in a shallow foam tray. Show how to press a potato tree in the paint, dab it on the tray to remove excess paint, then carefully print it on the white poster board. Allow the students to repeat this method with both shapes until they fill their forest.

# Clouds and Storms

## Ages 5-8

### Memory Verse

*Peace, be still. And the wind ceased.*

~Mark 4:39 KJV

## When Storm Clouds Arise

Do you like storms? Not many people do, but they are a part of nature. They occur when certain pressure fronts move in and collide with air currents, causing loud thunder and bright lightning. We can see a storm approaching when puffy, white clouds suddenly become fast-moving, black billows. It is necessary to seek shelter until the storm passes.

Sometimes in life things happen that are like storms. Everything seems dark and cloudy and we are afraid. We think that no one else sees our circumstances, but someone does see us and cares about what is happening. That someone is Jesus.

From time to time, even the disciples forgot that Jesus was in control of every situation. Once they were on a lake when a storm came up suddenly. The disciples panicked. Jesus was resting, so they quickly woke Him to ask what to do. Jesus spoke to the storm and the winds became calm. The disciples were amazed at His power.

Jesus is still in control today of every storm we encounter. If we look to Him for guidance, we can be assured that He will take care of us and safely guide us through whatever we have to face. We are His children and He loves us. We can seek shelter in His arms until our storms pass.

## For Discussion

**1.** What causes a storm?

**2.** Name some circumstances in your life that were "stormy."

**3.** Who is control of all storms?

# Clever Cloud Magnet

## What You Need

- cloud pattern from page 34
- white craft foam or white foam meat trays
- black or blue markers
- cotton balls
- magnets
- scissors
- glue

## Before Class

Duplicate the cloud pattern from page 34 for each child.

## What to Do

1. Show how to trace the cloud pattern on the foam and cut it out.

2. Have the students outline the cloud with a black or blue marker.

3. Help them write the memory verse in the center.

4. Allow the children to tear cotton balls into small pieces and glue them around the edges of the cloud, being careful not to cover the Scripture.

5. Give each student a magnet to glue to the back of the cloud (they may need two if the magnets are small).

Peace, be still. And the wind ceased. Mark 4:39

Make It • Take It • Make It • Take It • Make It • Take It • Make It • Take I

# Creation

## Ages 8-11

## Memory Verse

*In the beginning God created the heavens and the earth.*

~**Genesis 1:1**

## Days of Creation

Have you ever wondered how the world came to be? The Bible says in Genesis that God created the world. He made everything you see around you. On the first day, He made day and night. On the second day, He made air and clouds. On the third, He made the land and seas, grass, plants and trees. On the fourth day, He made the sun, moon and stars. On the fifth day, He made birds and fish. On the sixth, He made animals and man. Then on the seventh day, He rested. He made that day for us to worship Him.

And because God made it all, He is the owner. That means we belong to God, too, because He made us. Since He is the owner, He can do anything He chooses with us. We do not have the right to destroy our bodies with sinful things like drugs and alcohol because we don't own our bodies. Nor do we have the right to destroy other things in the world that God made.

God has given us the right to make choices. We must make sure that the choices we make will please the owner of the universe, God. Remember: we belong to Him.

## For Discussion

1. How did the world come to be?
2. What did God make on the sixth day?
3. Why don't we have a right to destroy our bodies?

**Make It** • **Take It** • **Make It** • **Take It** • **Make It** • **Take It** • **Make It** • **Take It**

# Fold-Out Creation Book

## What You Need

- booklet patterns from pages 37 and 38
- construction paper
- scissors
- crayons
- tape
- glue

## Before Class

Use the pattern on page 37 to cut a booklet cover from construction paper for each child. Duplicate the booklet pattern sheet from page 38 for each child.

## What to Do

1. Show how to fold the booklet cover in half like a book.

2. Have the students color the booklet pictures, then cut the page apart down the center solid line.

3. Show how to accordion fold the pages, taping the two strips together in a continuous accordion.

4. Instruct the children to glue the blank sheet to the inside front of the booklet cover.

5. Help the students write the memory verse on the back of the booklet.

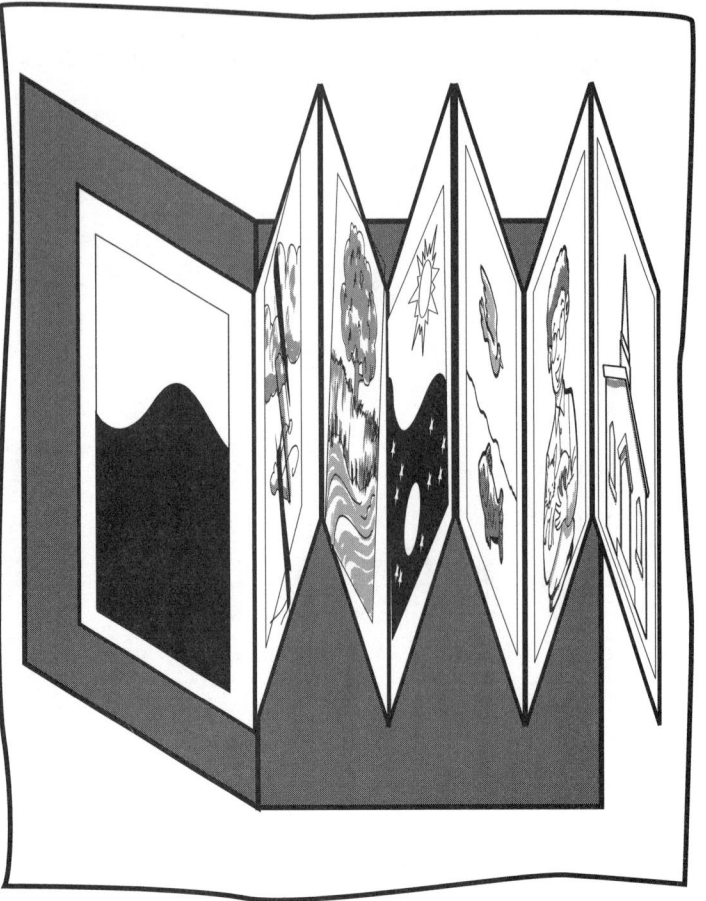

Make It • Take It • Make It • Take It • Make It • Take It • Make It • Take It

Days
of
Creation

38

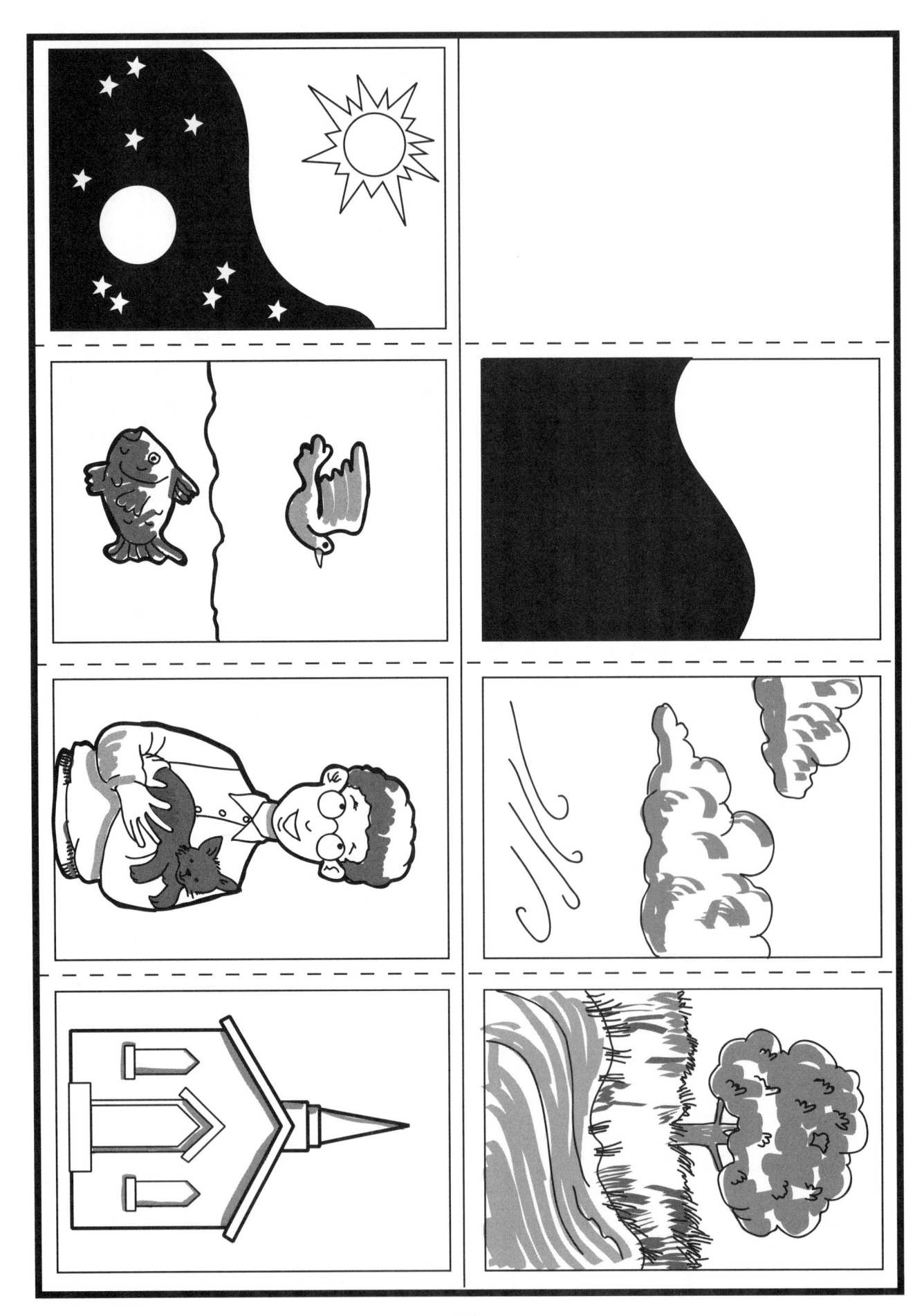

# Evergreen Tree

## Ages 8-11

## Memory Verse

*For God so loved the world that he gave his one and only Son, that whoever believes in him shall not perish but have eternal life.*

~**John 3:16**

## Everlasting Evergreens

Evergreen trees are easy to recognize because they look like traditional Christmas trees. They do not have leaves like most trees. Instead, they have thin, green needles. But unlike trees that lose their leaves in the fall, evergreens do not lose their needles. Evergreens have a nice pine smell. Balsam and spruce are two kinds of evergreens that make beautiful Christmas trees.

There is another kind of tree with needles but it is not an evergreen. It is called a tamarack. Sometimes people see tamaracks in the summer when they are full and green and assume they would make good Christmas trees, but when fall comes all the needles turn brown and fall off. The tamarack is no longer pretty.

The tamarack tree is like people who do not follow through in their commitment to Christ. Like the tamarack, these people look good for a while, but soon their ungodly behavior shows through and you see what they are really like when their ugly brown needles of sin start to show.

A true evergreen is always the same. It stays green for its entire life. God has given us the gift of everlasting life through His Son, Jesus. Don't be a tamarack Christian — stay beautiful in Christ, like the evergreen.

## For Discussion

**1.** What does an evergreen have instead of leaves?

**2.** How is a tamarack tree different from an evergreen?

**3.** How can you tell who is a committed Christian?

# Easter Grass Evergreens

## What You Need

- tree pattern from page 41
- white poster board
- green Easter grass
- brown construction paper
- glue or spray adhesive
- scissors
- markers

## Before Class

Duplicate the tree pattern from page 41 for each child.

## What to Do

1. Have the children use the tree pattern to cut a tree from white poster board.
2. Instruct them to cut a rectangle from brown construction paper and glue it to the trunk of the tree.
3. Have the children write the memory verse on the back of the tree with a marker.
4. Allow the children to snip the green Easter grass into small pieces.
5. Show how to apply glue or spray adhesive to the tree and sprinkle the grass liberally on it. Apply more glue if necessary and sprinkle grass again to make sure the entire tree is covered with "needles."

Make It • Take It • Make It • Take It • Make It • Take It • Make It • Take It

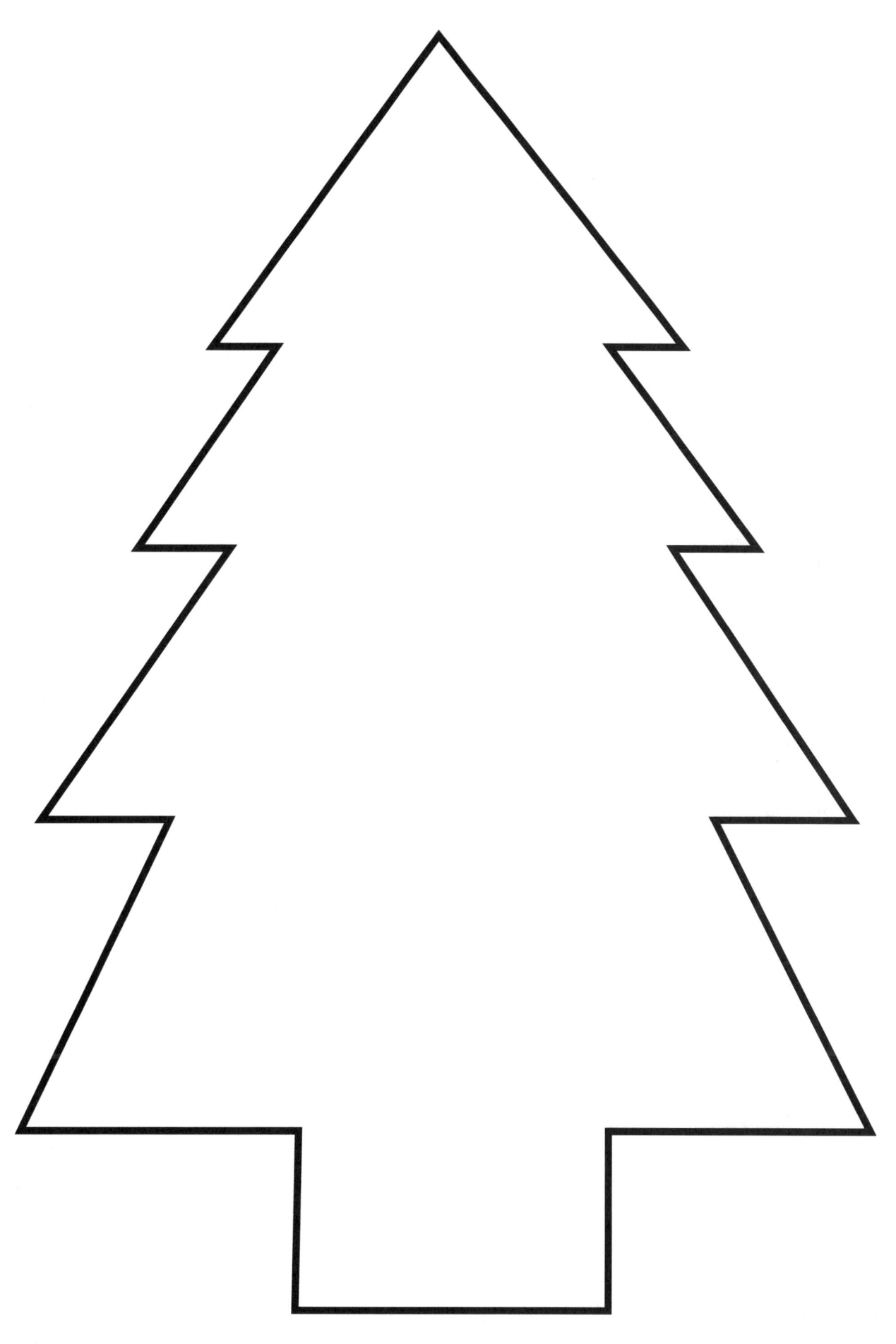

# Flower Gardens

## Ages 8-11

### Memory Verse

*Flowers appear on the earth; the season of singing has come.*

~Song of Songs 2:12

## Contented Flower Gardens

Flowers come in hundreds of varieties and colors. Some are large and bulky, like the sunflower, while others are tiny and delicate, like the violet. Some produce fruit or seeds while others are simply decorative. Some are crushed for making perfume.

In ancient times, flowers became symbols of national or religious sentiment. In Egypt, the lotus or water lily was associated with the supposed power of the Nile. The Indian lotus was sacred to the Hindus, who believed their God Brahma had been born in it. In ancient Greece, the olive wreath was given to victorious athletes. Flowers were also adopted by royal families as official emblems.

Flowers were also important in the Bible. Solomon mentions flowers in the Old Testament when he makes comparisons to our Lord: the lily of the valley (Song 2:1), the rose of Sharon (Song 2:1) and the apple tree (Song 2:3, 8:5).

When you walk through a flower garden and see and smell all the different kinds of flowers, you get a feeling of satisfaction. Jesus tells us to be content with small things. God created the flowers for our admiration and satisfaction.

## For Discussion

1. Name several different uses for flowers.
2. Which flowers are compared to Jesus?
3. What does it mean to be contented?

# Peaceful Promise Plants

## What You Need

- flower patterns from page 44
- cardboard
- construction paper
- small craft sticks
- single-serving cereal boxes
- brown paper
- scissors
- glue
- markers

*Flowers appear on the earth, the season of singing has come.*
*Song of Songs 2:12*

## Before Class

Use the flower patterns from page 44 to create templates from cardboard. Grocery bags work well for the brown paper used to cover the boxes.

## What to Do

1. Have each child use the templates to cut two flowers of each shape from any paper color they choose and six sets of leaves from green construction paper.

2. Help the children write a promise on each flower, such as, "I will clean my room," "I will feed the dog," etc.

3. Show how to glue each flower to a wooden craft stick.

4. Have the students glue the leaves on the sticks.

5. Assist the children as they cover a single-serving cereal box with brown paper.

6. Have the students write the memory verse on the side of the box.

7. Show how to cut six small slits on the top side of the box and encourage the children to "plant" their promise flowers.

43

# Fruit

### Ages 5-8

### Memory Verse

*By their fruit you will recognize them.*
           ~Matthew 7:16

## Spiritual Fruit

Do you like fruit? What makes it so appealing? Most fruit, when it is fully ripe, is sweet and leaves a pleasant flavor in our mouths after we eat it. It is also good for us. It provides vitamins and nutrients that we need for our bodies to grow strong and healthy. In countries where people do not get enough of the vitamins in fruit, they can become weak and sick from diseases.

In Galatians, we learn that if we do not have the fruit of the Spirit working in our lives daily, we will become sick with sinful nature. Some of these diseases are impurity, hatred, selfishness, jealousy, envy, idolatry and drunkenness.

The fruit of the Spirit are love, joy, peace, patience, kindness, goodness, faithfulness, gentleness and self-control. When we practice these fruit daily we will be appealing to those around us. Our words will be sweet and pleasant. Best of all, the sinful nature diseases will not be able to grow with the fruit of the Spirit inside us.

## For Discussion

1. How is fruit good for your body?
2. Name some "diseases" you can get if you do not eat spiritual fruit.
3. How can you get spiritual fruit?

Make It • Take It • Make It • Take It • Make It • Take It • Make It • Take It

# Juicy Fruit Match Game

## What You Need

- game card patterns from page 47
- heavy construction paper
- crayons or markers
- clear, self-stick plastic
- scissors
- glue
- zipper-style plastic sandwich bags

## Before Class

Duplicate two copies of the game card patterns from page 47 for each child.

## What to Do

1. Have the children color the fruit game cards with crayons or markers, using the appropriate colors.

2. Show how to glue each sheet of cards to a sheet of heavy construction paper.

3. Help the students cover the fruit sheets with clear, self-stick plastic.

4. Assist the children in cutting the sheets into cards. Give each student a sandwich bag in which to store the cards.

5. To play the game:
   Mix up all of the cards and lay them out face down on a table. Player one turns over two cards to see if they match. If they do, he or she keeps the pair. If they do not, he or she turns them back over and it is the next player's turn. When all matches have been made, the game is over and the player with the most sets wins.

Make It • Take It • Make It • Take It • Make It • Take It • Make It • Take It

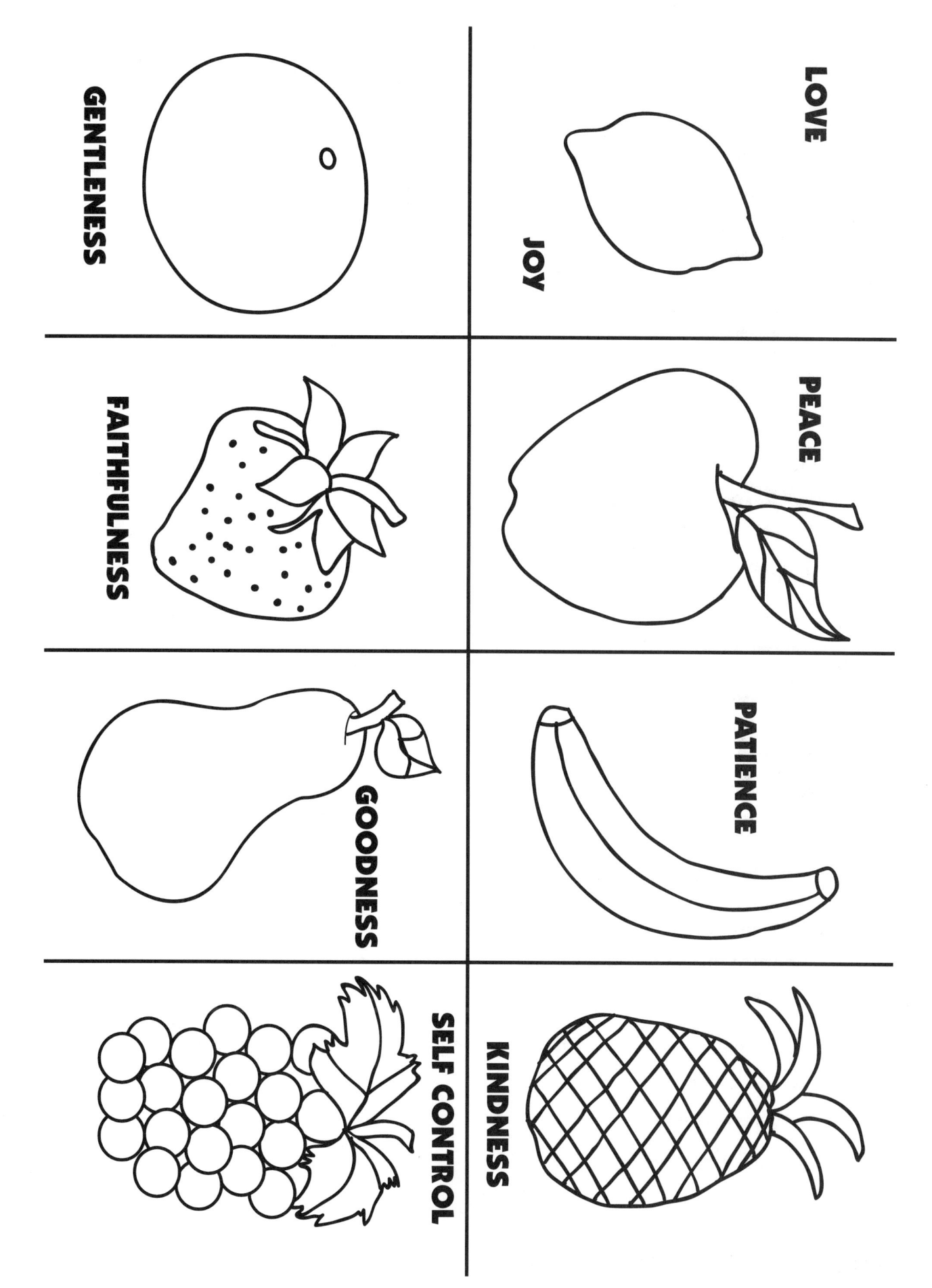

| LOVE | GENTLENESS |
|---|---|
| JOY | |
| PEACE | FAITHFULNESS |
| PATIENCE | GOODNESS |
| KINDNESS | SELF CONTROL |

# Garden of Eden

## Ages 5-8

## Memory Verse

*Awake to righteousness and do not sin.*
~1 Corinthians 15:34 KJV

## Sin in the Garden

God created a beautiful garden for Adam and Eve to live in. It was called the Garden of Eden. It was full of lovely flowers, rich vegetation and all kinds of splendid trees. Many of these were fruit trees that provided luscious fruit for Adam and Eve to eat. There was a river flowing through the garden to water the plants and trees. It was truly a magnificent place to live.

God provided a wonderful life for Adam and Eve with only one rule: do not eat from a particular tree in the middle of the garden. It was called the Tree of Knowledge of Good and Evil. God warned Adam and Eve that if they ate from that tree, they would surely die.

Things went well for a time, but then one day that old tempter — Satan — appeared as a snake and talked Eve into eating from the forbidden tree. Then Eve gave Adam fruit to eat from that tree, and they committed the first sin. God sent them away from the beautiful garden. Adam and Eve had to work hard for everything after that.

Satan is still around today, trying to tempt others into sinning. He probably told Eve that one little bite wouldn't hurt, just like he might tell us that one little lie, or one little stolen candy bar, can't hurt us. Don't be fooled! A sin is a sin and all sin is wrong. It will lead to destruction for us just like it did for Adam and Eve in the Garden of Eden.

## For Discussion

**1.** Describe the Garden of Eden.

**2.** Who lived there?

**3.** Why were they told to leave?

**4.** What was the source of their sin?

# Forbidden Fruit Trees

## What You Need

- tree patterns from page 50
- cardboard
- green and red construction paper
- scissors
- markers

## Before Class

Cut several cardboard templates of the tree and apple using the patterns on page 50.

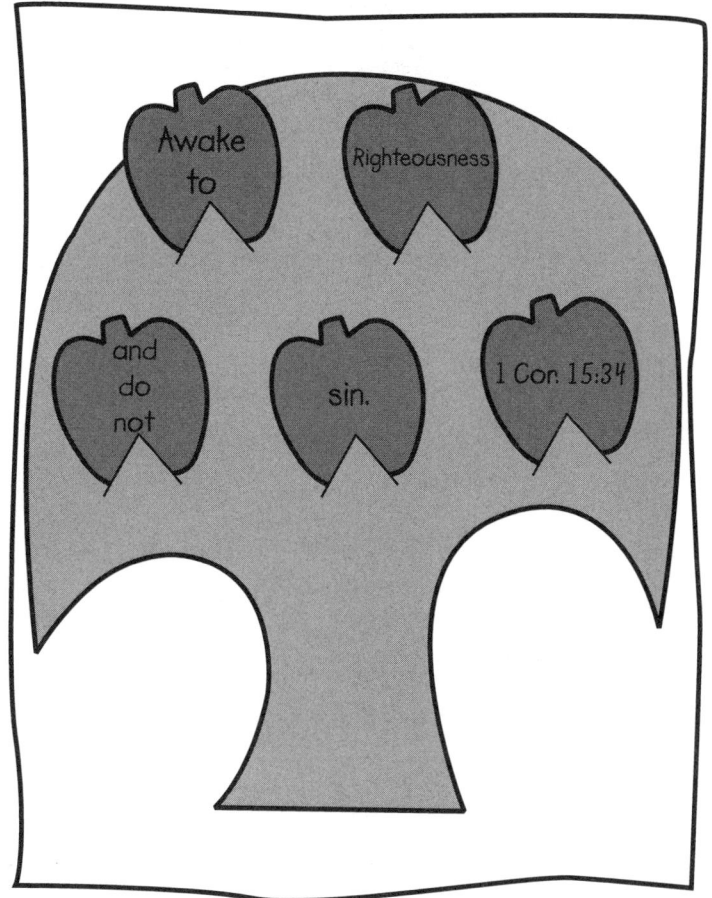

## What to Do

1. Let the children trace the tree onto a folded sheet of green construction paper.

2. Show how to cut out the tree, being careful not to cut the fold.

3. Have the students use the pattern to trace five apples on red construction paper and cut them out.

4. Help the children write the memory verse on the apples.

5. Show how to cut five inverted "V" slits in the tree and slide one apple in each.

6. Encourage the children to mix up the apples on their tree and have a friend try to place them in order.

*Make It · Take It Crafts*

49

# Lily of the Valley

## Ages 8-11

## Memory Verse

*I am a rose of Sharon and a lily of the valleys.*

~Song of Songs 2:1

## Sweet Lilies of the Valley

The lily of the valley is one of the sweetest smelling flowers God made. Even its appearance is sweet and fragile-looking.

Lilies of the valley will bloom in the shade. They like to nestle down in the shady part of a yard or garden so that they may go unnoticed, but their sweet aroma gives their hiding place away. They respond well to being transplanted into other areas. One plant will grow many new plants until a whole area is filled.

The Song of Songs compares Jesus to a lily of the valley. We know He had some very sad or shady times in His life when people were not always kind to Him, but instead of bitterness, His sweetness came through.

He was transplanted (moved from one spot to another). First He was in heaven, then His Father sent Him to earth. When He died and rose again, He went back to His Father, leaving behind the many "plants" — or believers — that would one day be transplanted to heaven also. If you are a Christian and have asked Jesus into your heart, you are one of the lilies He planted!

## For Discussion

1. Describe a lily of the valley flower.
2. How did Solomon compare Jesus to one?
3. How can we make our "sweetness" known to others?

# Fragile Tissue Lilies

## What You Need

- stem and leaf pattern from page 53
- green and brown construction paper
- white tissue paper
- scissors
- glue
- pencils
- markers

> I am a rose of Sharon and a lily of the valleys.
>
> Song of Songs 2:1

## Before Class

Duplicate the stem and leaf pattern from page 53 for each child.

## What to Do

1. Have the students use the pattern to cut two sets of leaves and stems from green construction paper.

2. Show where to glue the stems toward the bottom of the brown paper.

3. Instruct the children to cut the white tissue paper into tiny squares, just big enough to wrap around the end of a pencil.

4. Show how to place the eraser end of a pencil in the center of a single tissue square and pull the paper up around it evenly. Gently crush it to form a cup. Do not pull the pencil out.

5. Demonstrate how to dip the covered end into a small dab of glue and place it along the stem to make tiny flowers. Repeat until both sides of each stem are filled from about halfway up to the top.

6. Have the students write the memory verse in the center of the picture.

53

# Moon

### Ages 5-8

### Memory Verse

*God made two great lights.*

~**Genesis 1:16**

## One Great Light

People have always been intrigued by the moon. So much, in fact, that they have built space ships that will take them to the surface of the moon to explore it.

When we think of the moon, we often associate it with all the darkness that surrounds it, rather than the light it reflects. But in the Bible, Genesis tells us that God made two great lights: the greater to rule the day — the sun — and the lesser to rule the night — the moon. The purpose was to separate light from darkness.

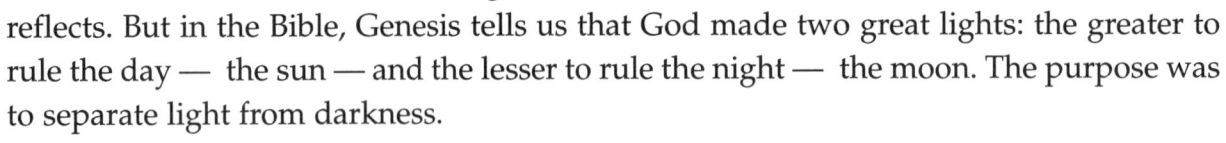

A night sky should remind us that when all seems dark and frightening, God has provided a light to shine forth in our lives, too. We need only to look for His light by praying, reading the Bible and going to church to meet with other Christians and learn more about Him.

## For Discussion

**1.** Why are people so interested in the moon?

**2.** Why did God create the moon?

**3.** Of what can a night star remind us?

**Make It • Take It • Make It • Take It • Make It • Take It • Make It • Take It**

# Marble Painted Moon

## What You Need

- moon pattern from page 56
- 9" x 12" black construction paper
- yellow construction paper
- black tempera paint or poster paint
- aluminum pie pans
- marbles
- scissors
- glue
- white chalk
- hair spray
- foil stars

*God made two great lights.*
*Genesis 1:16*

## Before Class

Duplicate the moon pattern from page 56 for each child.

## What to Do

1. Have each child trace and cut a circle from yellow paper using the moon pattern.

2. Show how to roll a small piece of tape into a circle, then use the tape to attach the circle to the center of the pie pan.

3. Help the students dip a marble into black paint and drop it onto the circle. Assist as they roll the marble across the circle several times. The marble may be redipped and repeated if necessary, but don't cover the entire surface.

4. Allow the circle to dry slightly.

5. Show how to glue the circle to black construction paper.

6. Have the students write the memory verse below the circle using white chalk. A light spritz of hair spray will keep the chalk from flaking off.

7. Allow the children to attach star stickers around the moon.

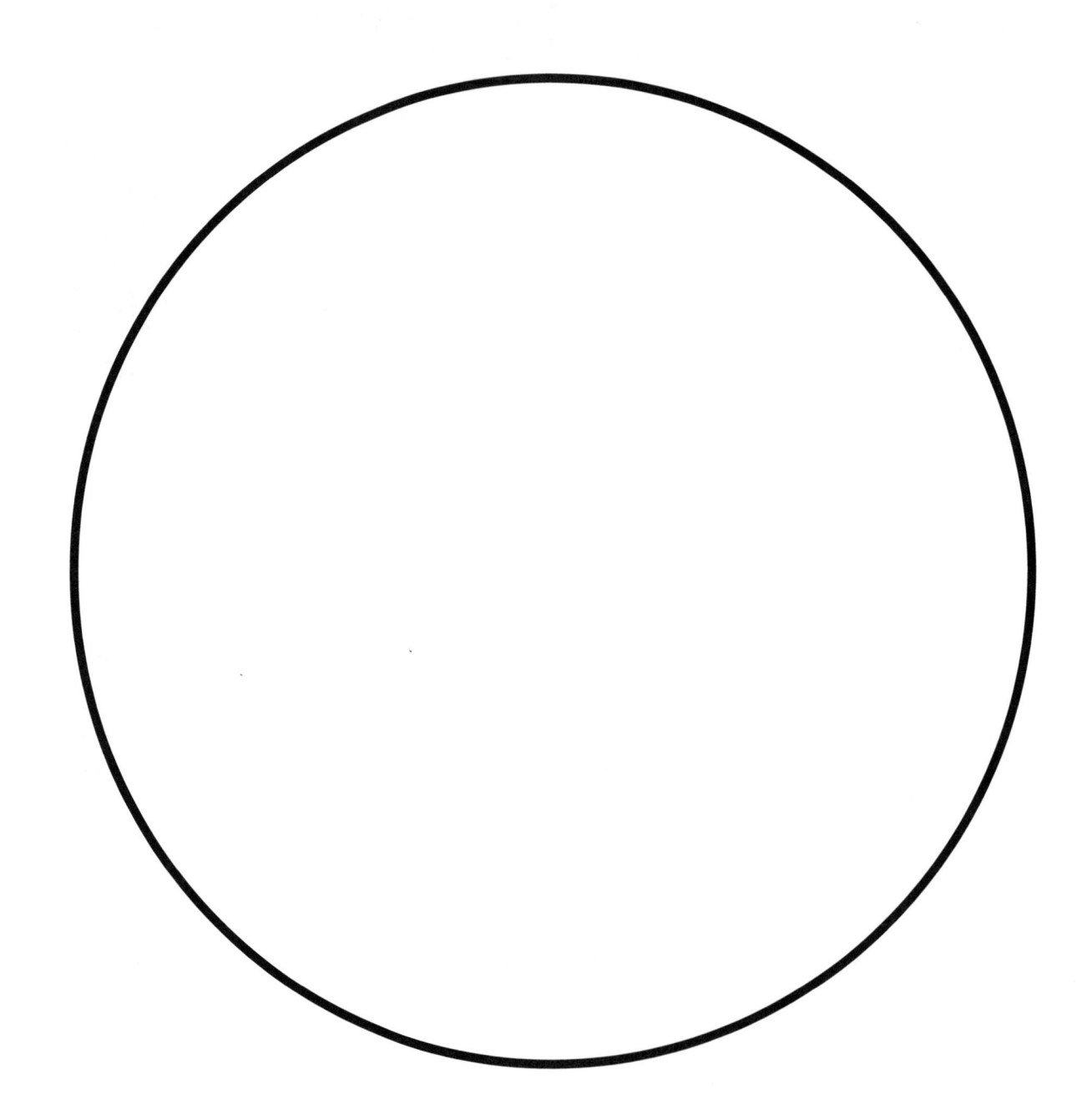

# Palm Tree

### Ages 5-8

### Memory Verse

*They took palm branches and went out to meet him, shouting, "Hosanna!"*

~John 12:13

## An Important Palm

Palm trees have a single trunk with no branches and are topped with a tuft of fan-like leaves. They grow in tropical or subtropical climates. Maybe you have seen them if your family has been to a beach on vacation. Palm trees are quite different than any other type of tree, yet they are very useful because almost every part is valuable for something.

The coconut and date palms produce delicious fruit. Palm oil has become an important source of vegetable oil used in making margarine and soap. The seeds of the palm are made into food for camels. The fibers are woven into ropes and riggings. The tall trunk is used for lumber. The fan-like leaves are used for decorative purposes. In Bible times, the leaves were a symbol for victory.

Like the palm tree, we have many parts that can be useful for God. We can use our lips to sing praises and witness to others. We can use our hands to do service for those in need as God has instructed in His Word, the Bible. Or you may use your hands to play an instrument to glorify God. Our feet can take us to church on Sunday to worship. Most of all, we can give our hearts to Jesus and then all of our parts will be able to work for Him.

## For Discussion

**1.** Where do palm trees grow?
**2.** Name some of the uses for palm trees.
**3.** What parts of us can be used for God and how can they be used?

Make It • Take It • Make It • Take It • Make It • Take It • Make It • Take It

# Cut 'N' Twist Palm Tree

## What You Need

- paper towel tubes
- brown paper
- green construction paper
- broom handle
- glue
- scissors
- markers

## Before Class

Construction paper or paper bags work well for the brown paper.

## What to Do

1. Have the students cover the outside of a paper towel tube with brown paper and glue it on securely.

2. Help the students roll a 12" x 18" sheet of green construction paper tightly around a broom handle, then slide it off the handle still holding it securely.

3. Show how to make four or five cuts from the top of the rolled paper to about halfway down.

4. Assist the children in smearing the bottom half of the rolled paper with glue and placing it into one end of the paper towel tube, allowing the roll to expand inside the tube.

5. Show how to use a pencil to curl the ends of the palm branches down.

6. Allow the students to make scattered black slash marks around the tree trunk with a black marker.

7. Write or have the children write the memory verse toward the bottom of the tree.

# Raccoon

**Ages 5-8**

**Memory Verse**

You shall not steal.

~Exodus 20:15

## The Robbing Raccoon

The raccoon is a furry little woodland creature known as a "bandit." Raccoons are called bandits partly because of the black mask-like lining around their eyes and partly because of their common way of obtaining food: they steal it. Raccoons are known to rob eggs from bird and turtle nests. The raccoon constantly prowls to find small, unsuspecting animals. A raccoon will go into an area where people live to steal food and garbage. Raccoons have very nimble fingers that can turn door knobs and open refrigerators. They work mostly at night.

The Bible has very specific instructions about stealing. One of the Ten Commandments that God gave says, "You shall not steal." Anytime you take something that does not belong to you, no matter how small it is, that is stealing! Stealing is a sin.

We can also make a comparison between Christians and raccoons by how the raccoon prefers to do its prowling at night. The Bible says in John 3:19, "Men loved darkness instead of light because their deeds were evil." Don't take on the habits of a raccoon, who steals and prefers darkness. Live in the light, doing only what is good and pleasing to the Lord.

## For Discussion

1. Why is a raccoon known as a bandit?
2. What do raccoons steal?
3. When do raccoons like to work?
4. Why do people prefer darkness?

# Robber Raccoon Mask

## What You Need

- raccoon patterns from page 61
- brown and black construction paper
- yarn
- scissors
- glue
- markers
- hole punch

## Before Class

Duplicate the raccoon patterns from page 61 for each child. Cut yarn into 12" lengths, two per child.

## What to Do

1. Have the children use the pattern to cut two head pieces from brown construction paper and two eye pieces from black paper.

2. Show how to glue an eye piece on each head piece.

3. Help the students cut out the eye holes.

4. Allow the children to color the nose tips black and outline the mouth with marker.

5. Show how to fold the head pieces in opposite directions, placing the nose pieces flat against each other.

6. Allow the students to glue the two head pieces together along the top nose edge from the bottom of the ear to the end of the black tip. Do not glue the mouth area.

7. Have the students punch a hole on each side of the mask and attach a piece of yarn to each side.

8. Have the students write the memory verse inside the mask.

61

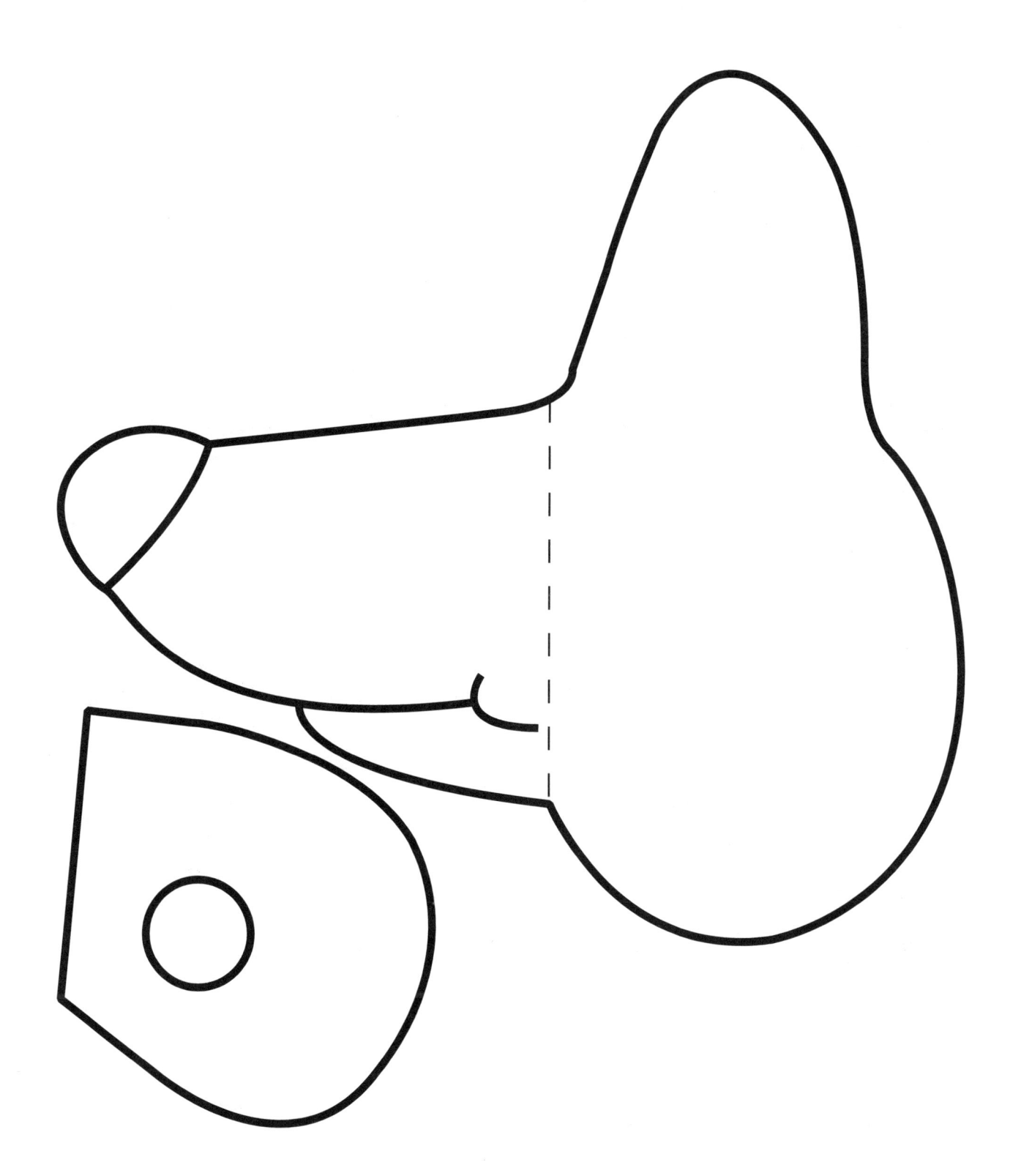

# Rain

### Ages 5-8

### Memory Verse

*You gave abundant showers, O God.*
~**Psalm 68:9**

## Replenishing Rain

What good is rain? It spoils our picnics, it spoils our ball games and it certainly spoils a parade! We could just do without rain forever, right? No, we can't! If we didn't have rain, we couldn't eat because no crops would grow. We wouldn't have any beautiful flowers to smell. Without rain, the lakes, rivers and streams would dry up and the fish would die. Every living thing needs rain.

The Bible tells about places where it didn't rain for years and how the land withered and dried up. But when God sent the rain, it replenished the earth. Replenish means "to make full again."

Sometimes, people become like a land without rain. We may not feel physically thirsty but if we are not drinking from God's Word every day, we can dry up inside. We need to read our Bibles and talk to God to replenish our souls. Just like a rain shower replenishes the earth so it can grow, we must keep our lives full of God so we can grow.

## For Discussion

1. What are the benefits of rain?
2. What does "replenish" mean?
3. How can we replenish our lives?

**Make It • Take It • Make It • Take It • Make It • Take It • Make It • Take It**

# Colorful Cut 'N' Glue Umbrellas

## What You Need

- umbrella patterns from pages 64 and 65
- cardboard
- construction paper
- scissors
- glue
- markers

## Before Class

Use the patterns on pages 64 and 65 to cut cardboard templates of the umbrella pieces for the children to trace on construction paper.

## What to Do

**1.** Have the children trace and cut out the umbrella pieces on the paper colors of their choice.

**2.** Show how to glue the three top sections of the umbrella to the umbrella base.

**3.** Have the students trace and cut one umbrella handle from brown construction paper and glue it to the center bottom of the back of the umbrella.

**4.** Write the memory verse or have the students write it on the umbrella with a marker.

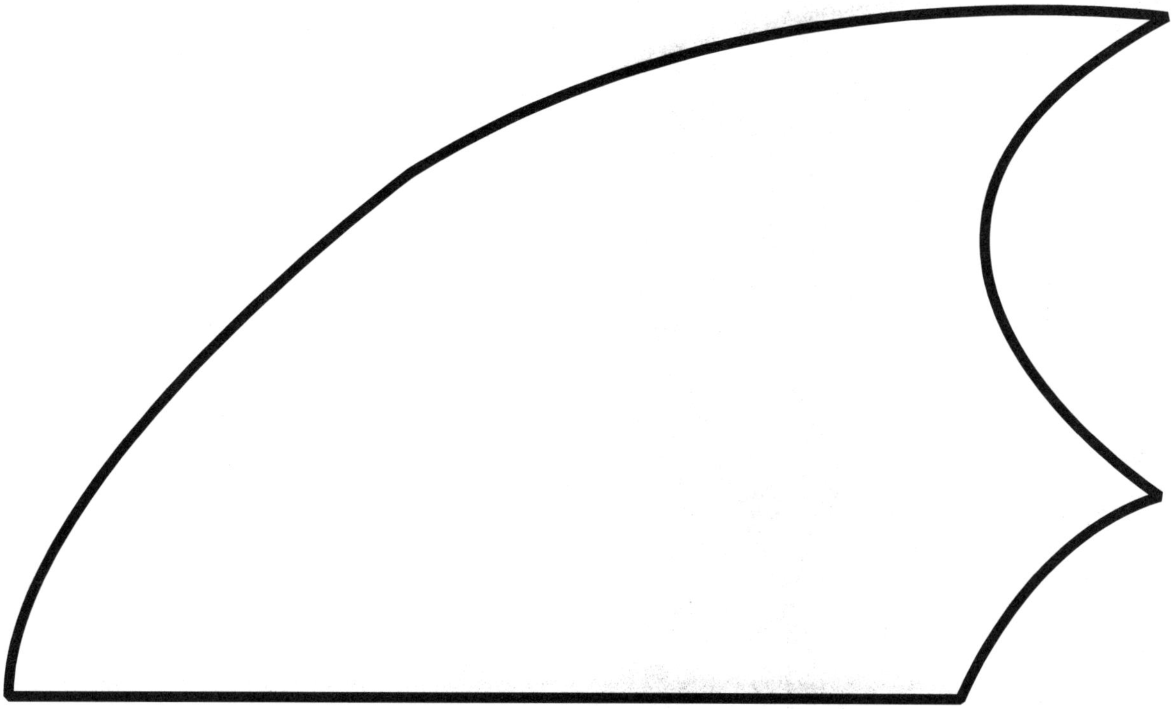

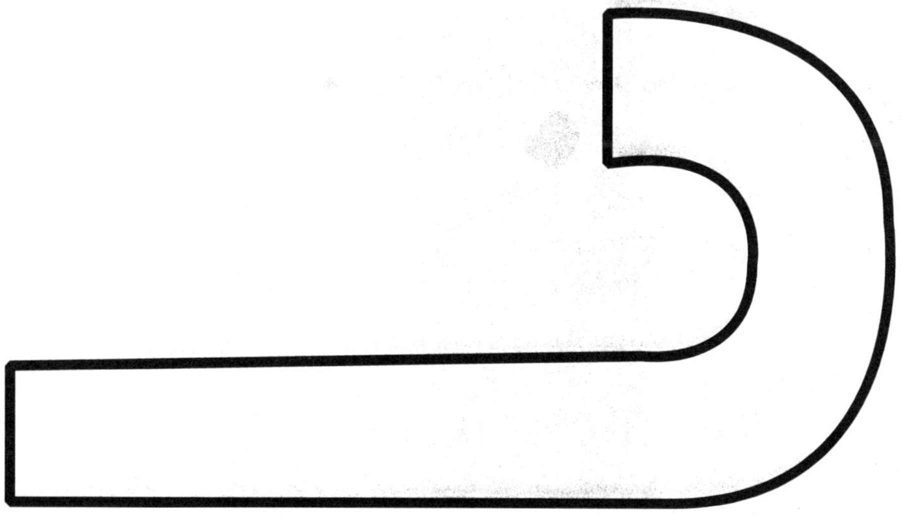

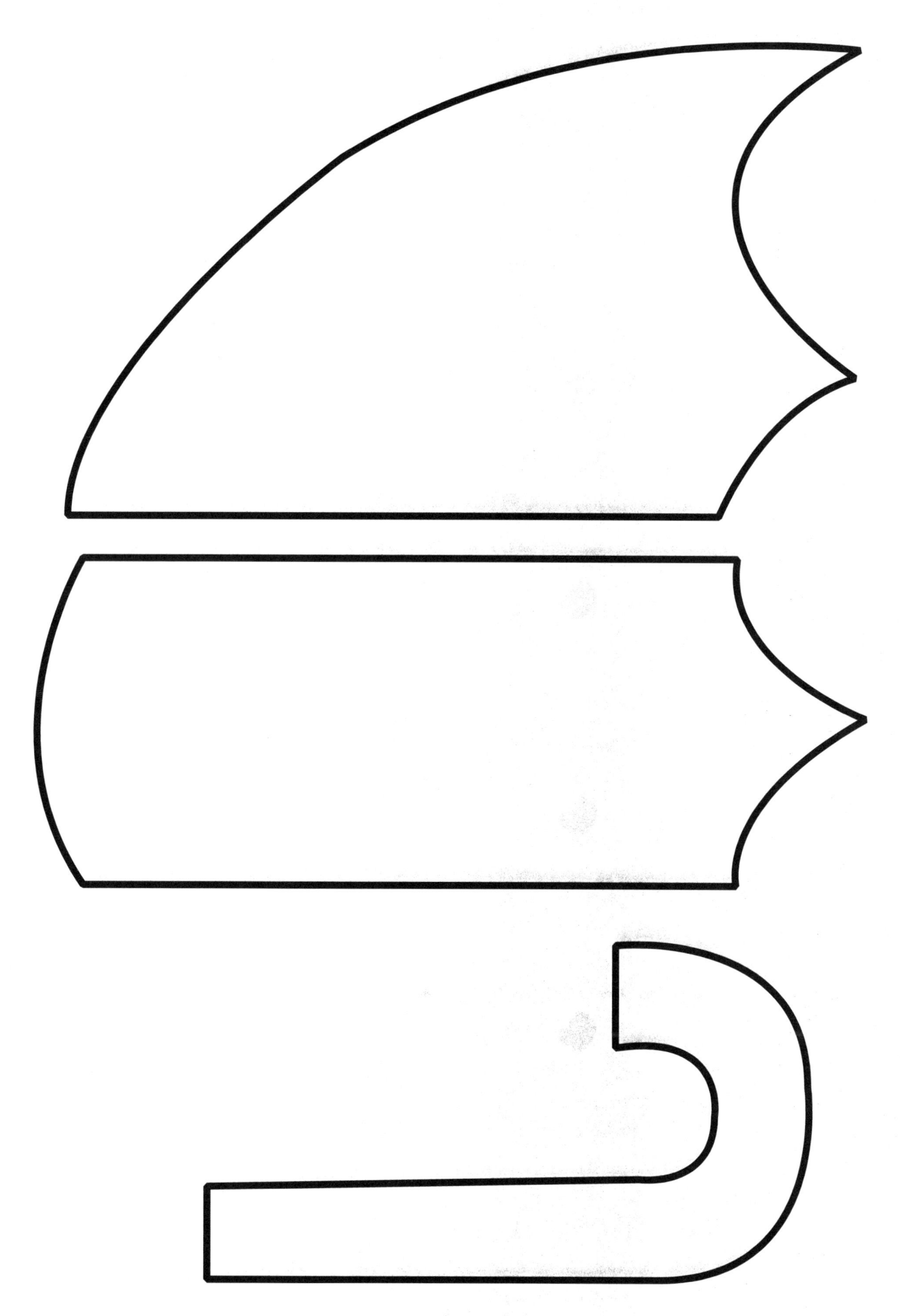

# Rainbows

### Ages 8-11

### Memory Verse

*I have set my rainbow in the clouds.*
~Genesis 9:13

## Rainbows of Promise

A rainbow is an arch of light that exhibits a spectrum of colors. It is caused by drops of water falling through the air. Rainbows are usually in the sky opposite the sun. We may see them at the end of a rain shower, but sometimes they are visible in the spray of a waterfall.

When you see a rainbow, your first reaction might be to admire the beautiful colors that span across the sky. But did you know that the rainbow was created to remind us of God's promises? In Bible times, when the world was so wicked that it had to be destroyed, God found one righteous man: Noah. Before the Flood, He told Noah how to build an ark so Noah and his family could be spared. God instructed Noah to take two of every kind of creature on the ark. After the Flood was over, God placed a rainbow in the sky as a sign of His promise to never again destroy the whole earth with a flood.

God has many other promises in His Word for us. He promised to never leave us, to provide for our needs, to comfort us and to love us. When you see a rainbow in the sky, let it remind you of all of God's promises.

## For Discussion

**1.** What causes a rainbow?
**2.** Of what is the rainbow a reminder?
**3.** Name some other promises God gives.

**Make It • Take It • Make It • Take It • Make It • Take It • Make It • Take It**

# 3-D Tissue Rainbow

## What You Need

- rainbow pattern from page 68
- white poster board
- yellow, blue and pink tissue paper
- glue
- pencils
- markers
- scissors

## Before Class

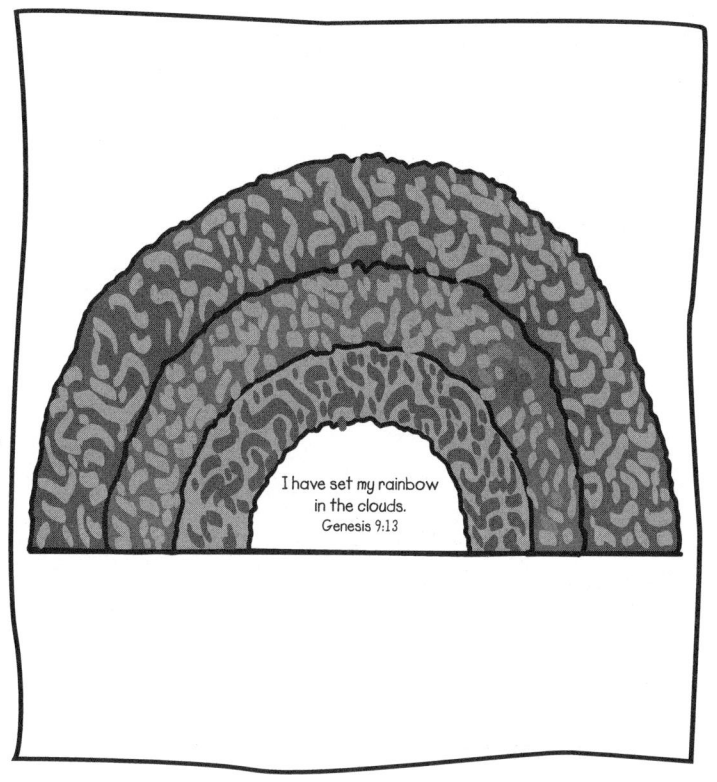

Place the rainbow pattern from page 68 on folded paper, then trace and cut it out. Unfold the rainbow and draw the lines across it. Make several for the students to use as templates.

## What to Do

1. Have the students use the template to trace the rainbow on poster board.
2. Instruct the children to draw in the lines with a marker.
3. Have the students write the memory verse on the lower center of the rainbow.
4. Allow the children to cut the three colors of tissue paper into 1" squares. They will need many of each color!
5. Show how to fill a small section of one stripe on the rainbow with glue.
6. Demonstrate how to place the eraser end of a pencil on the center of a tissue square, then bring up the edges and crush it around the pencil. Set the tissue down lightly in the glue and carefully pull the pencil end out. Have the students repeat this method until one rainbow stripe is entirely covered with one color. Encourage the children to pack the tissue tightly together so no white poster board is exposed.
7. Have the students repeat the same procedure with the other two colors on the remaining stripes.

Note: This is a time consuming project but the end results are worth the extra time. If you choose to do this project with younger children, have them crumple the tissue squares one at a time with their fingers and glue to the rainbow instead of using the pencil method.

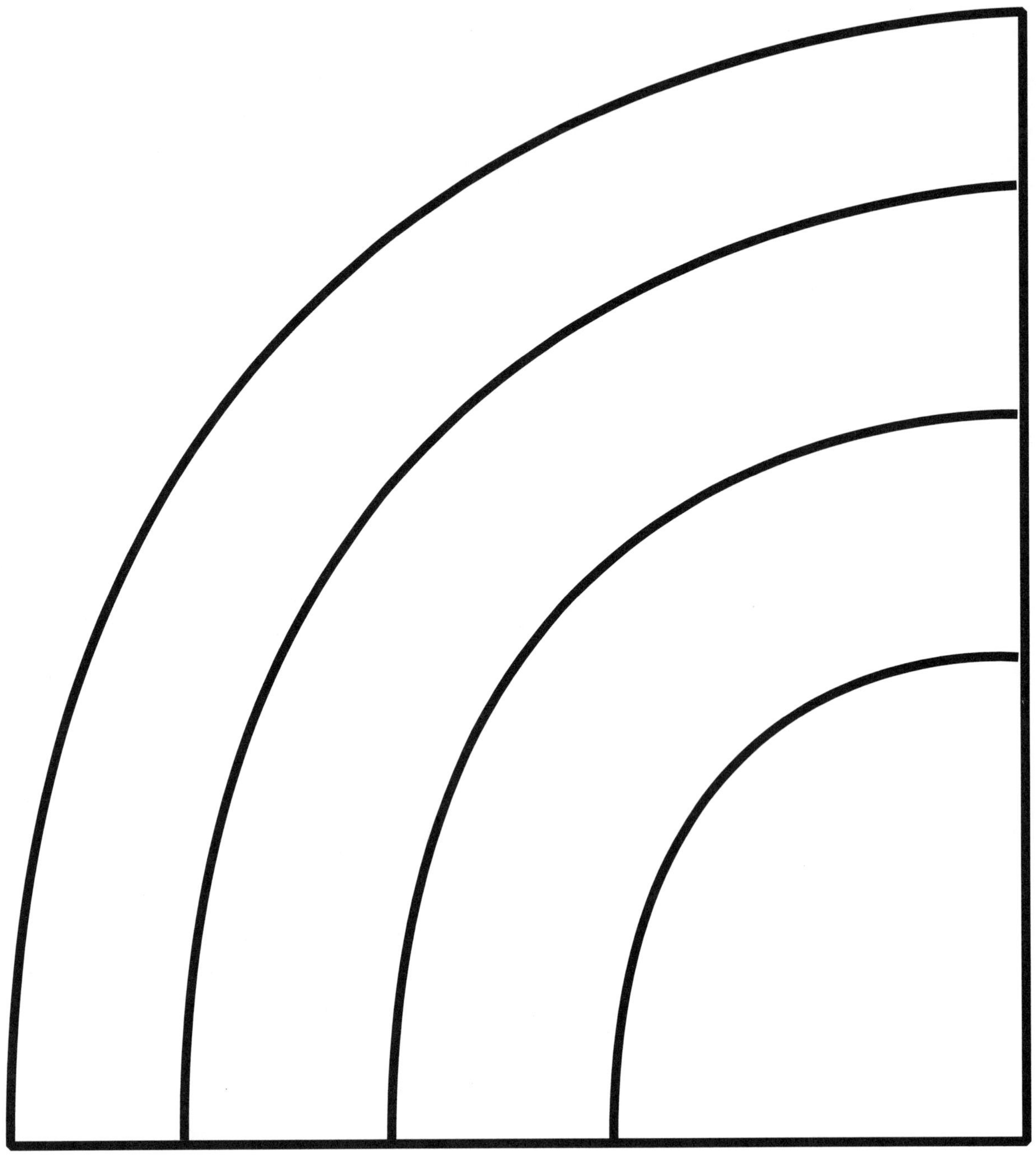

# Rocks

## Ages 8-11

## Memory Verse

*He alone is my rock and my salvation.*
~Psalm 62:2

## The Solid Rock

Everyone knows what a rock looks like. (Show several sizes and colors.) The term actually refers to any naturally-formed collection of minerals. They are divided into three categories depending on their origin. Nevertheless, we know one thing about rocks: they are hard! You can't break them with your bare hands, you can't crack them with your teeth (at least you shouldn't try to!) and you can't bend them. They are solid!

Because of their strength, rocks make an excellent building material for foundations. You can cement them together to make retaining walls and dams. While massive amounts of water might eventually move rocks, it still cannot break them.

Many places in the Bible refer to Jesus as our Rock and our Salvation. Just as small animals hide in the rocks for safety, we can take refuge in our Rock, Jesus. If we have our hope in God, then our foundation is built on a solid rock. Storms and trials can't break us when we are securely standing on the Rock. Our Rock is Jesus.

## For Discussion

1. Describe a rock.
2. For what are rocks useful?
3. How is Jesus like a rock for us?

**Make It • Take It • Make It • Take It • Make It • Take It • Make It • Take It**

# Rock Head Family

## What You Need

- foam plates
- rocks (assorted sizes)
- fine-tip permanent markers
- craft glue
- hole punch

## Before Class

Punch a hole in the top center rim of each plate for hanging.

## What to Do

**1.** Give each child a foam plate.

**2.** Write or have the children write the memory verse toward the top of the plate, leaving plenty of space for the rock family.

**3.** Have a selection of rocks from which the children can select rocks to make "people" (one medium size rock for a head, one large rock for the body, two pebbles for feet, etc.).

**4.** Show how to use a fine-tip marker to draw clothes and faces on the rock family.

**5.** Help the students glue the rocks to a foam plate with craft glue.

**6.** Allow plenty of drying time before the students take the plate home.

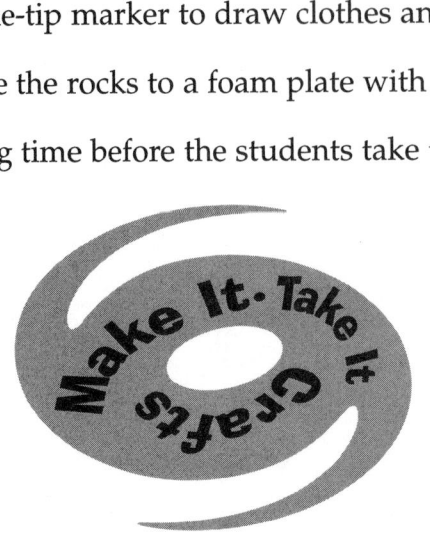

*He alone is my rock and my salvation. Psalm 62:2*

Make It • Take It Crafts

# Roses

### Ages 8-11

### Memory Verse

*The desert shall rejoice, and blossom as the rose.*

~Isaiah 35:1 KJV

## Fragrant Roses

Roses are one of the best-known flowers. Almost everyone has seen a rose. It is an important flower because it is used in bouquets and corsages. On New Year's Day, you have probably seen on TV thousands of beautiful roses used to decorate floats in the Tournament of Roses Parade.

The rose adds color to a garden and makes the whole garden more attractive. The rose is fragrant. It sends out an aroma to everyone around it. People like to be near roses because they look and smell so pleasant.

In the Bible, the Song of Songs says, "I am the rose of Sharon" (Song 2:1). Jesus is like the rose. He is beautiful, even though we can't see Him. He adds beauty to our lives. People around us can see the peace, happiness and joy in us when we have Jesus as our Savior — His love makes us beautiful, too.

Jesus also makes our lives fragrant. People will want to be around us when our lives give off the pleasant aroma of being a Christian. We can do this through kindness, gentleness and love.

Live the fragrant life of the rose of Sharon!

## For Discussion

**1.** For what are roses used?

**2.** Why are roses considered pleasant?

**3.** How is Jesus like a rose?

# Fold 'N' Peel Roses

## What You Need

- leaf pattern from page 73
- tissue paper
- green chenille wire
- green construction paper
- scissors
- glue
- markers
- perfume

## Before Class

Duplicate the leaf pattern from page 73 for each child.

## What to Do

**1.** Have the students cut 12-16 pieces of tissue paper into 6" x 9" rectangles. They should stack them together, then start at the longer side and accordion-fold the stack in small folds.

**2.** Help the children pinch the stack together in the center, flattening the center folds, and secure them by tightly wrapping a green chenille wire around it a couple of times.

**3.** Instruct the students to begin separating the sheets of tissue one at a time by gently peeling them toward the center. (Caution the children that the paper will tear very easily if is not handled gently.)

**4.** They should continue separating the sheets until they are all separate and the rose looks full.

**5.** Have the students cut one set of leaves from green construction paper using the pattern.

**6.** Instruct the children to write the memory verse on the leaves.

**7.** Show how to drop a line of glue down the center of the leaves and attach it to the stem.

**8.** Allow the children to add a drop or two of perfume to the rose for fragrance.

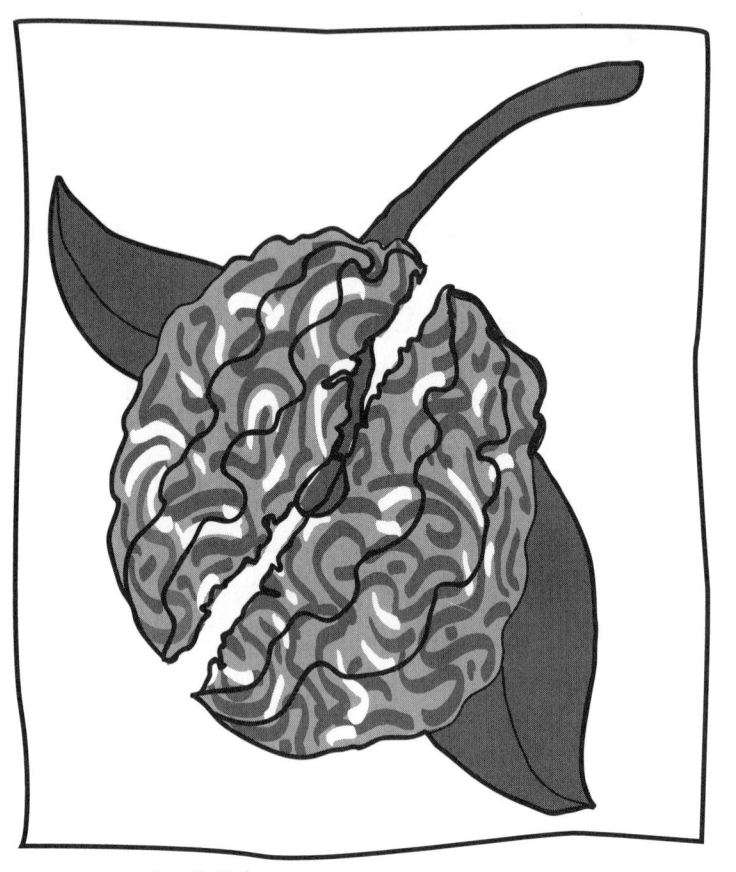

# Springs

### Ages 8-11

### Memory Verse

*Indeed, the water I give him will become...a spring of water welling up to eternal life.*

~**John 4:14**

## Refreshing Springs

A spring is a natural flow of water that comes from the ground at a single point within a restricted area. A spring can emerge on dry land or in beds of streams, ponds or lakes. The cold springs that supply bottled water are a result of rainfall that has soaked into the ground and emerged as a spring at some other point on a lower level. The water pressure becomes so great that the water is forced to the surface, causing a spring of clear, cold, refreshing water.

Have you ever been outside on a very hot day and gotten so thirsty that all you could think about was getting some water? Do you remember how cool and refreshing that glass of water tasted? It quenches your dry mouth and throat and makes you feel alive again!

Jesus asked a woman standing by a well to give Him a drink of water. Then He told her that anyone drinking from an ordinary well would get thirsty again, but if people drink from the Living Water it would be like a spring constantly welling up inside of them. Jesus is the Living Water. By looking to Him, we receive peace and assurance to keep our souls from ever becoming thirsty again.

## For Discussion

1. From where does a spring come?
2. Describe spring water and how it tastes.
3. Who is the Living Water?

**Make It • Take It • Make It • Take It • Make It • Take It • Make It • Take It**

# Hanging Bottle Planter

## What You Need

- bottle pattern from page 76
- cardboard
- empty two-liter soda bottles
- utility knives or sharp scissors
- hole punch
- yarn
- clear, self-stick plastic
- markers

*Indeed, the water I give him will become...a spring of water welling up to eternal life. John 4:14*

## Before Class

If you have a younger, less skilled group, you might want to pre-cut the bottles (see steps below). If the students will be cutting the bottles, use the pattern to make cardboard templates for them to trace. Cut yarn into twelve 12" lengths per child.

## What to Do

1. Show how to trace the template around the bottle four times.

2. Assist the students in using a utility knife or sharp scissors to cut away the top portion. They should use a hole punch in each of the four tabs as shown on the pattern.

3. Have the children write the memory verse on a 5" x 5" piece of paper. They may add any decorations you provide or color it in any way.

4. Show how to lay the verse on the bottle and cover it with a 9" x 6" piece of clear self-stick plastic.

5. Help the students braid the yarn together in sets of three and tie a double knot in one end.

6. Show how to slide the other end of the yarn through one of the holes in the planter tabs. Tie all four braids securely together at the top of the planter.

7. Explain that a small plant can be placed in the container and the wells at the bottom of the bottle will hold extra water.

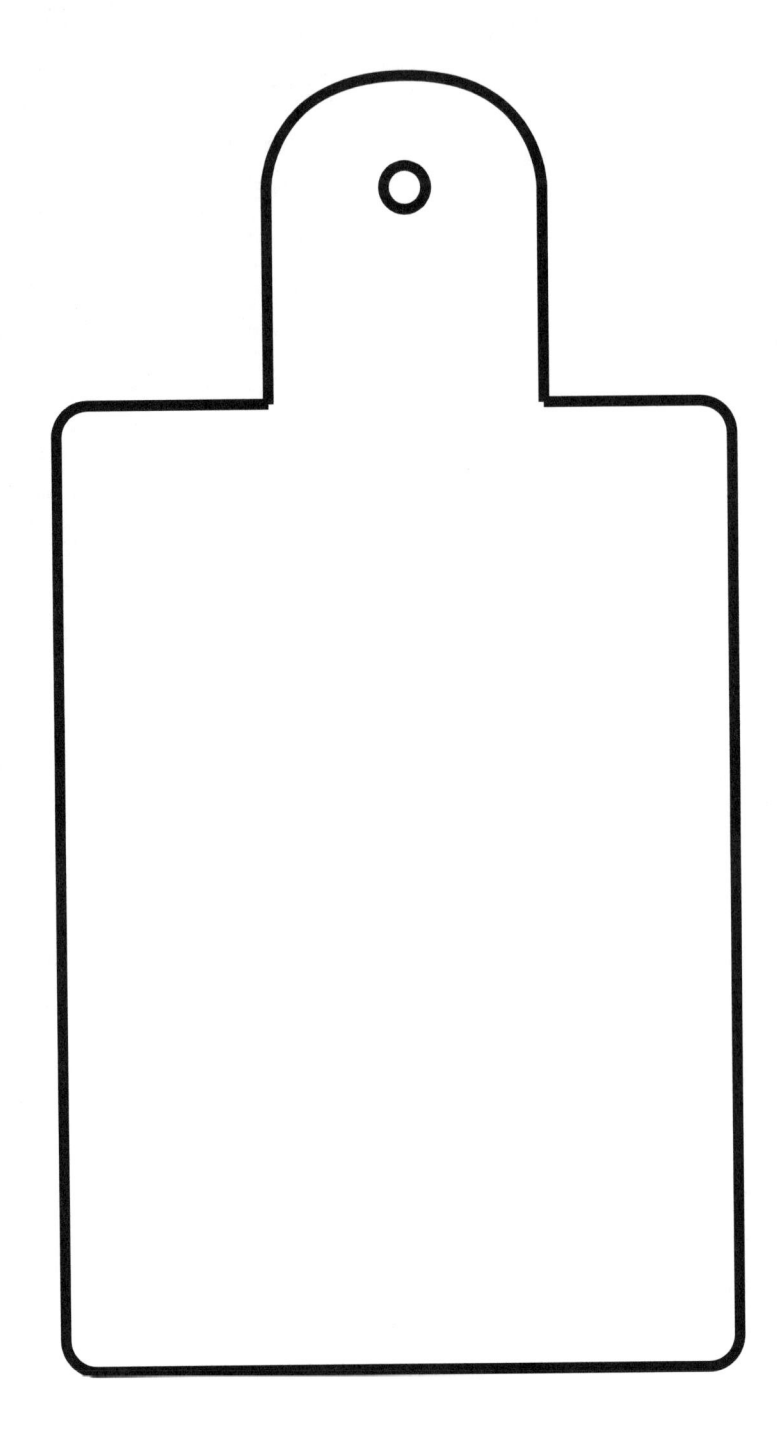

# Stars

### Ages 8-11

### Memory Verse

*When they saw the star, they were overjoyed.*
~Matthew 2:10

## Signs in the Stars

Have you ever looked up in a clear night sky and tried to count all of the stars? How far did you get? There are about 8,000 stars that are visible to the naked eye, but not all at one time. The sun, of course, is the largest star and dominates the sky during the daytime. With the exception of the sun, stars appear to be fixed, maintaining the same pattern year after year. But they are actually in rapid motion. Stars are so far away from us that the changes in position become apparent only over centuries.

Ancient astronomers studied the stars. They tried to identify and chart the stars. They made predictions by reading the placement of the stars in the sky. They used the stars to foretell signs of things to come. Stars are beautiful, but they cannot predict our lives, even though some people still try to say they do. Only God knows what will happen in our lives.

Perhaps the most well-known star is the one that hung over the stable in Bethlehem the night Jesus was born. It shone so brilliantly that it drew attention from miles around. Later it moved across the sky to lead the wise men to baby Jesus. Just like the rest of His creation, God can use stars to draw us closer to Him.

## For Discussion

**1.** Why did the ancient astronomers study the stars?
**2.** Describe Bethlehem's star and its purpose.
**3.** Who is the one true Light?

# Shining Star Mobile

## What You Need

- star patterns from pages 79 and 80
- heavy yellow construction paper
- cardboard
- glitter
- plastic drinking straws
- scissors
- glue
- markers
- hole punch
- string
- ornament hooks
- stapler

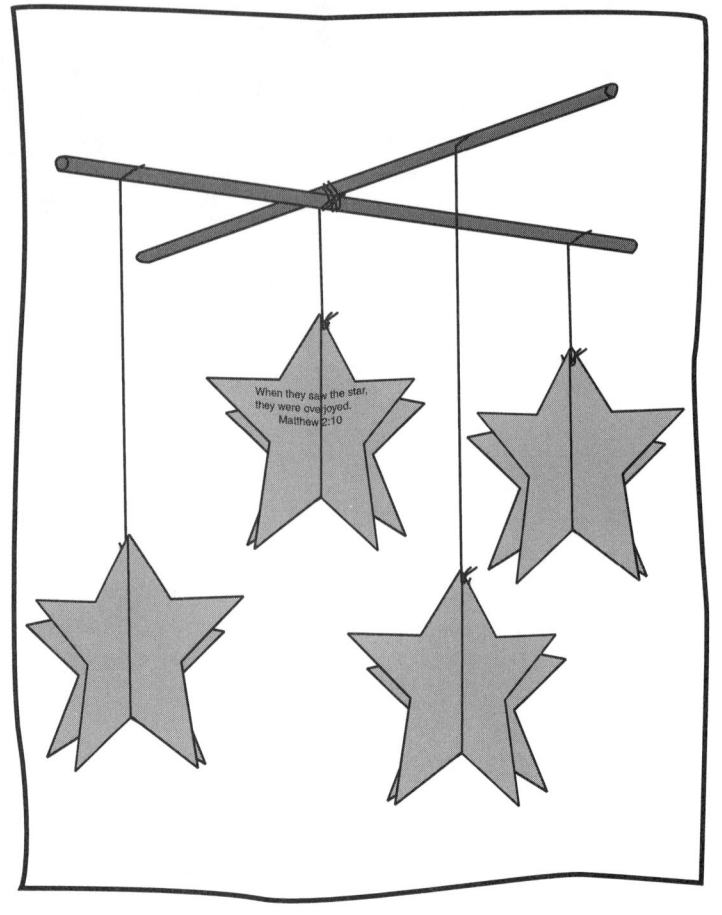

## Before Class

Duplicate the star patterns from pages 79 and 80 and trace all four on cardboard to make templates.

## What to Do

1. Have the children trace two of each size of star on yellow or gold construction paper and cut them out.

2. Instruct the students to write the memory verse on one star with a marker.

3. Show how to cut each of the other stars halfway up, then slide one of the same size onto it. Drop a small line of glue along the cut to hold it in place.

4. Allow the students to lightly smear glue on each set of stars and sprinkle them with glitter.

5. Show how to place two plastic straws crisscross on each other and staple them in the middle.

6. Help the students to punch a hole in each star set, thread string through and tie the stars around the ends of the mobile.

7. Assist the students in tying a wire ornament hook to the center of the straws with string.

8. Show how to attach the memory verse star hanging from the center of the mobile.

78

# Sun

## Ages 8-11

### Memory Verse

*Do not let the sun go down while you are still angry.*

~Ephesians 4:26

## Not So Sunny!

Did you know that the sun is actually a huge star? It consists mainly of hydrogen. Near the center of the sun, the temperature is 29,000,000°F. By gravitation, the sun dominates the planetary system, including earth. Using the radiation of its energy, the sun directly or indirectly supports life on earth because food and fuel come from plants that use sunlight.

Throughout time, the sun has been regarded by humans as having special significance. Ancient cultures worshipped the sun. Many recognized it as important to the cycle of life. But it has perhaps most commonly been used as a tool to measure time. The sun's appearance in the morning and disappearance in the evening can always be depended on.

In Ephesians, when Paul was teaching the people how to live as "children of the light," he discussed anger. Using the sun as a guideline, he encouraged the Ephesians to not let the sun go down while they were still angry with someone, because the longer they harbored anger against each other, the easier it would be for Satan to take control.

If we are angry with someone we should go to that person and ask forgiveness. Work out the problem before you go to bed at night. Holding anger inside overnight will only make the problem bigger. Get rid of your anger before the sun goes down each day. Use the sun as a reminder to check your life for wrong attitudes and hidden anger.

## For Discussion

**1.** Describe the sun.

**2.** For what did ancient cultures use the sun?

**3.** Why shouldn't we go to bed angry?

# Sun Catcher Sun

## What You Need

- sun patterns from page 83
- yellow tissue paper
- clear, self-stick plastic
- glitter
- scissors
- hole punch
- small squares of paper
- yarn
- markers

## Before Class

Duplicate the sun patterns for each child from page 83. Cut an 18" x 30" sheet of clear, self-stick plastic for each child.

## What to Do

1. Have the students cut out the patterns and use them to cut one circle and 10 triangles from yellow tissue paper.
2. Assist the children in laying the plastic sheet lengthwise on a table and peeling back most of the backing, leaving the sticky side up.
3. Show how to place the triangles carefully in a circle with the tips touching. You might want to instruct the students to arrange the triangles beside the plastic first to get an idea of the pattern before placing them on the sticky plastic where they cannot be moved.
4. Have the students place the yellow circle in the center of the triangles.
5. Allow them to sprinkle the sun with glitter.
6. Instruct the children to write the memory verse on a small piece of paper and place it below the sun.
7. Show how to carefully pull off the rest of the contact paper covering, then pull the remaining side over the sun picture, smoothing out wrinkles and air bubbles as much as possible.
8. Allow the students to trim the edges of the plastic to any shape they choose.
9. Show how to punch a hole in the top of the plastic and use yarn for hanging the sun in a window.

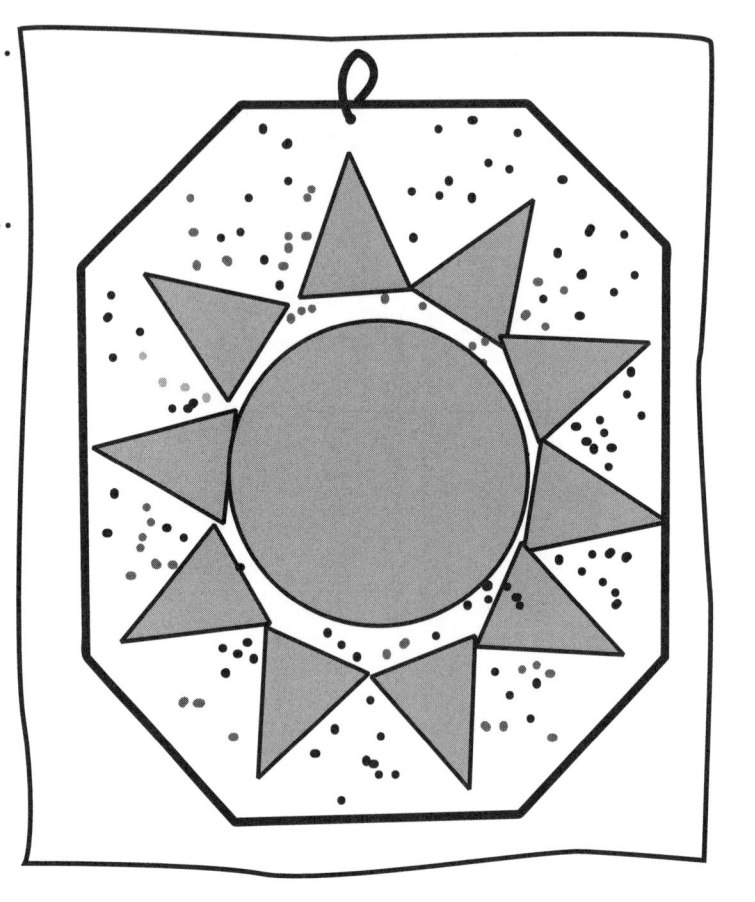

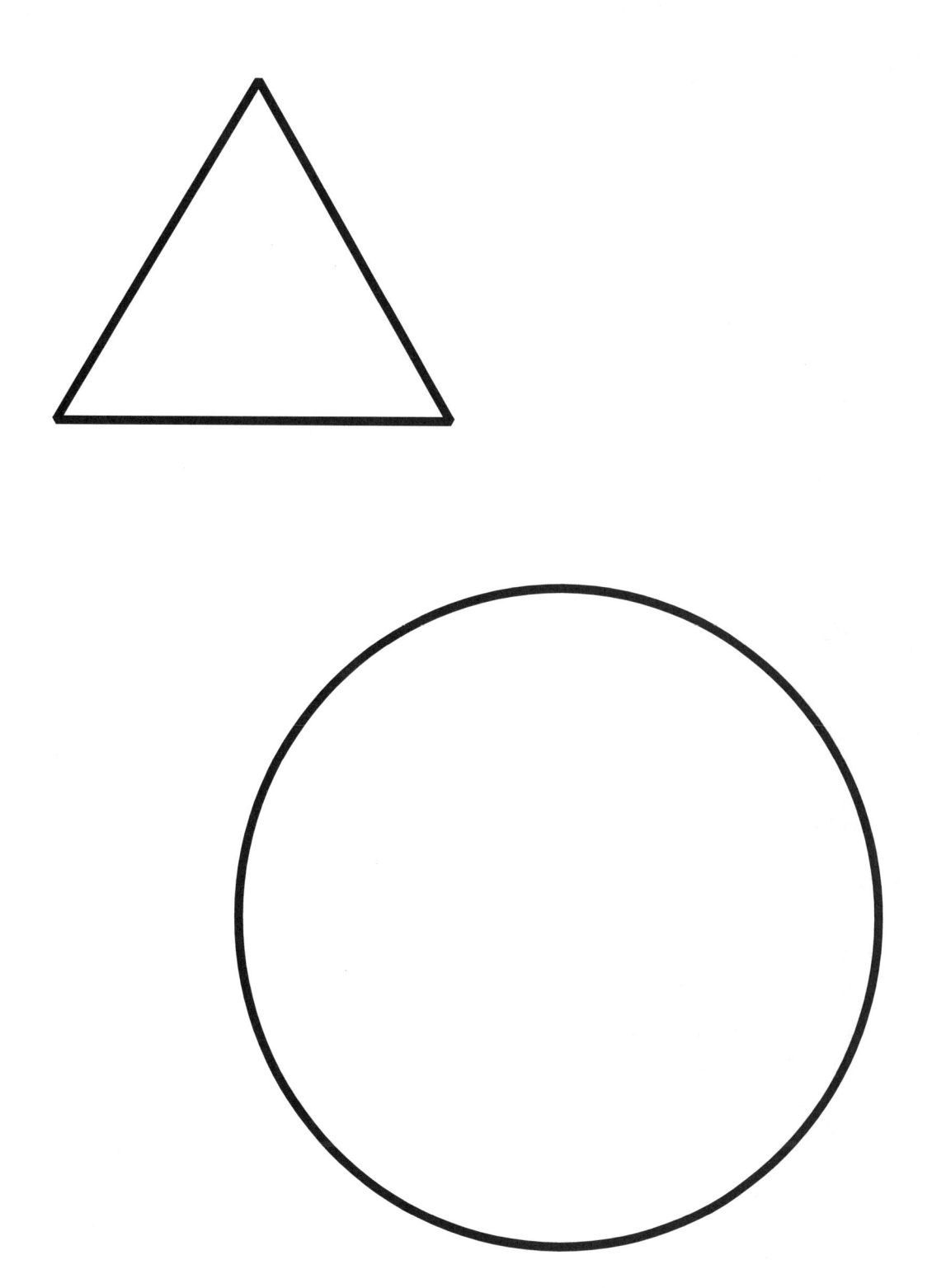

# Sunflower

**Ages 8-11**

## Memory Verse

*The Lord will be my light.*

~Micah 7:8

## Sturdy Sunflowers

Have you ever gotten up early in the morning and looked at a flower garden? There is a tall, sturdy flower with pointed yellow petals and a thick black center that you should notice. It is called a sunflower. When the sun is coming up in the east, the sunflower will turn to face that direction. But when you see a sunflower at noon, it will be tipped up because the sun is directly overhead. Sunflowers seem to slant their "faces" in the direction of the sun. They need that light!

In the Bible, when Peter saw Jesus walking on water, he wanted to come to Him. Jesus told him to come, so Peter stepped out of the boat. As long as Peter kept his eyes on the "Son" he was fine, but when he looked down, he began to sink.

We can learn a lesson from the sunflower. If we turn our eyes on God's Son we will be safe, but if we look away as Peter did, we will sink into sin. We need the light in our lives. Keep your eyes on the Son!

## For Discussion

1. Why does the sunflower face the sun?
2. What happened when Peter took his eyes off Jesus?
3. Why do we need the "Light" in our lives?

Make It • Take It • Make It • Take It • Make It • Take It • Make It • Take It

# Fold 'N' Cut Sunflowers

## What You Need

- patterns for sunflower from page 86
- yellow, brown and green construction paper
- scissors
- glue
- markers
- hole punch
- tape

## Before Class

Duplicate the sunflower patterns from page 86 for each child.

## What to Do

1. Have the students fold a 9" x 12" sheet of yellow construction paper in half.
2. Show how to cut from the fold upward, making several 5 1/2" cuts.
3. Have the children open and hold the paper lengthwise, attaching the two top edges together with tape and then the two bottom edges.
4. Show how to flatten the paper into a sunflower with the "petals" sticking out.
5. Allow the children to place a drop of glue inside each set of petals and hold them firmly to secure.
6. Have the students use the pattern to cut two brown circle centers.
7. Instruct the children to write the memory verse on one center, then glue one to each side of the sunflower (the centers will protrude).
8. Have the students use the patterns to cut a stem and leaves from green construction paper then glue them to the sunflower.
9. Allow the children to punch a hole in the top center petal so they can hang their giant sunflower.

# Tares and Weeds

### Ages 5-8

### Memory Verse

*Let both grow together until the harvest.*
~**Matthew 13:30**

## Sorting Weeds and Tares

Jesus tells a story in Matthew 13:24-30 about a man who planted a wheat field. When it started to grow, the man could see that there were tares — or weeds — among the wheat. His servants asked if they should go out and pull up the tares, but the man said, "No, because you might uproot the wheat with them. Leave them alone until harvest time and then we will separate them. We will bundle the weeds and burn them and we will gather the wheat into my barn."

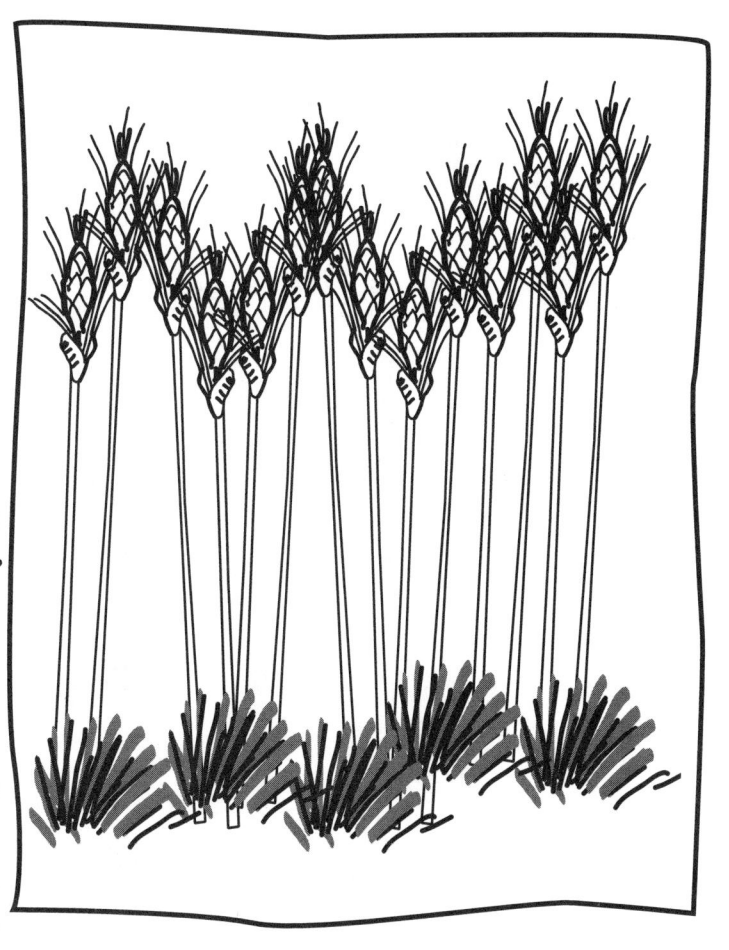

This could be a parable about people. There are good people and there are bad people in the world. Sometimes it is hard for us to distinguish between them because some bad people can put on good appearances. But Jesus said when it is harvest time it will be easy to recognize the sinners from the Christians and then they will be separated. Each one will get his or her reward for the kind of life he or she lived.

## For Discussion

**1.** Why didn't the man want the weeds pulled out right away?
**2.** How were they going to separate the weeds from the wheat?
**3.** How are some people like weeds and what is their reward?

Make It • Take It • Make It • Take It • Make It • Take It • Make It • Take It

# Weeds Jigsaw Puzzle

## What You Need

- picture and puzzle guide from pages 89 and 90
- crayons or markers
- poster board
- clear, self-stick plastic
- scissors
- glue or spray adhesive
- zipper-style plastic sandwich bags

## Before Class

Duplicate the picture and puzzle guide from pages 89 and 90 for each child.

## What to Do

1. Allow the children to color the sheet with crayons or markers.
2. Help the students glue the sheet to poster board (spray adhesive works best).
3. Assist the children in covering the picture with clear, self-stick plastic.
4. Show how to trace the puzzle guide on the back by pressing a pencil into the poster board.
5. Allow the students to cut apart the puzzle pieces.
6. Give the students a sandwich bag in which to carry their pieces.

Make It • Take It • Make It • Take It • Make It • Take It • Make It • Take It

**Let both grow together until the harvest.
Matthew 13:30**

90

# Tree by Water

## Ages 5-8

## Memory Verse

*He is like a tree planted by streams of water.*

~Psalm 1:3

## A Tree by the Water

Have you ever seen the roots of a plant? They are long, tubular masses that go down deep into the ground. The roots absorb water and nutrients that the plant needs to grow.

The roots of a tree are larger and stronger than those of a smaller plant but the purpose is the same. When a tree is planted near a source of water, the roots go deep to absorb that moisture continually to grow a powerful, steadfast timber. It will not be easily shaken by the elements around it.

In Psalm 1, the Bible compares a righteous person to a tree planted by the water. Just like the watered tree will give fruit and not wither but prosper, if a Christian draws strength from the Living Water, Jesus Christ, the storms and situations we face daily won't be able to knock us down. When we read and meditate on God's Word, our roots go deeper and become stronger in knowledge. We won't go the way of the wicked because Christ will be our source of immovable strength.

## For Discussion

**1.** What is the purpose of roots?
**2.** How do deep, strong roots help a tree?
**3.** How can we have strong roots and how will they help us?

Make It • Take It • Make It • Take It • Make It • Take It • Make It • Take It

# Towering Tree Sponge Painting

## What You Need

- tree patterns from page 93
- green and brown construction paper
- white poster board
- green tempera paint
- sponges
- blue tempera paint
- foam meat trays
- clothespins
- scissors
- glue
- markers

*He is like a tree planted by streams of water. Psalm 1:3*

## Before Class

Duplicate the tree patterns from page 93 for each child. Also cut a leaf shape and a triangle shape from a sponge for each child.

## What to Do

**1.** Have the students trace and cut a tree top from green construction paper and a tree trunk from brown construction paper.

**2.** Show how to glue these to a 9" x 12" piece of poster board.

**3.** Write or have the students write the memory verse at the side of the tree.

**4.** Pour a small amount of green paint on a meat tray. Show how to use a clothespin to hold the leaf sponge, then dab it in the paint and touch it to the tree top to make foliage.

**5.** Then show how to pinch the triangle sponge with a clothespin and dab it in blue paint. Paint water under the tree across the bottom of the poster board. Do not stroke or brush, simply dab.

# Vine

## Ages 5-8

### Memory Verse

*I am the vine, you are the branches.*

~John 15:5

## A Fruitful Vine

A vine is a slender, creeping or climbing plant. Vines grow to be big and strong. Some vines grow fruit on their branches, like grapes. If the branches are cut from the vine they will die. They won't produce any fruit. The branches need the strength of the food that the vine gives.

Jesus said He is like a vine and we are like the branches. He gives us strength and helps us to grow more loving, patient, kind and forgiving.

To become a branch of the true vine, Jesus, we must ask Jesus to forgive our sins and then tell Him we want to obey Him. We can be as close to Him as a branch is to a vine.

## For Discussion

**1.** Describe a vine and name some things that grow on vines.

**2.** Why is the vine important to the branches?

**3.** Why do we need the "true vine"?

*Make It. Take It Crafts*

# Fruitful Grape Clusters

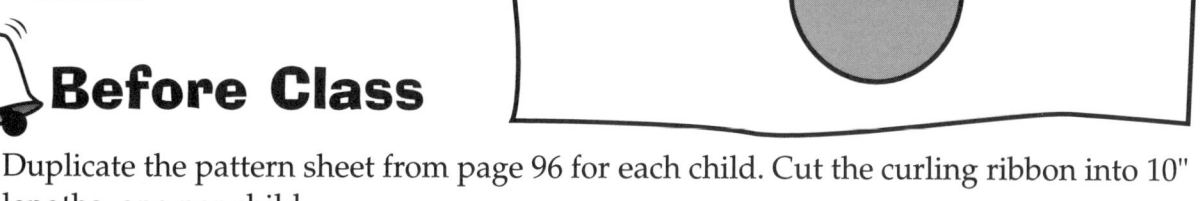

## What You Need

- grape patterns from page 96
- poster board
- construction paper
- green curling ribbon
- scissors
- glue
- markers

## Before Class

Duplicate the pattern sheet from page 96 for each child. Cut the curling ribbon into 10" lengths, one per child.

## What to Do

**1.** Have the children use the triangle pattern to cut one from poster board.

**2.** Have the students use the grape pattern to cut 10 from purple construction paper.

**3.** Have the children use the leaf pattern to cut two from green construction paper.

**4.** Have the students use the pattern to cut one stem from brown construction paper.

**5.** Show how to glue the grapes, overlapping, to the cluster base starting with a row of 4, then 3, then 2 and then 1.

**6.** Allow the students to glue the stem to the top of the cluster.

**7.** Assist the children as they use scissors to curl a piece of green curling ribbon. After curling, they should carefully snip one end of the ribbon and tear it down the center lengthwise into two curls. They should glue one curl to each side of the stem.

**8.** Have the students glue on the leaves.

**9.** Write or have the students write the memory verse on the grapes.

96